# World War I Diary of Private Brooks on the Western Front.

**Trench photo by Ernest Brooks.**

(**Title Page**)

The day to day diary of an infantry private in the trenches during the Great War for Civilisation, August 1914 to November 1918. (A new publication)

A true objective story by Private William Brooks.

Complemented by official narratives and newspaper articles of the time. Maps and some photographs in public domain. Bearing in mind that there were rest periods, leave periods and that he could only be at one place in a small part of the line, this narrative reflects the nature of the war on the Western Front, warts and all.

**Copyright Page**

# World War I Diary of Private Brooks on the Western Front.



ISBN 978-0-9576489-0-6 : POD Paperback version at www.amazon.co.uk

Date of first publication : 21 May 2013.

Publisher : PeterPJD Publishing.

Also available as

ISBN 978-0-9576489-1-3 eBook-Kindle at www.Amazon.co.uk

and as eBook-PDF: ISBN 978-0-9576489-2-0 at www.cdbooks-r-us.com

**Preface** :
Will Brooks was born in the district of All Saints, in the city of Birmingham on the 16th of January, 1880, the youngest of a family of three. He left school at the age of 13 and worked with an old family friend, as a carrier with a horse and cart, providing a daily service between Birmingham and Warwick. At the age of 18, whilst in Birmingham, he joined the Royal Warwickshire Regiment to serve an initial regular engagement of 7 years with the colours, to be followed by 5 years in the reserve.

**Will Brooks the writer**

His service with the colours was extended to 8 years, whilst overseas. In 1911, at the termination of his reserve service - he was reengaged as a class D reservist, under the reserve forces and Militia Act, to serve a further 4 years. Six of his eight years' service with the colours, were spent overseas in Malta, Bermuda, Gibraltar and South Africa.

During his period in reserve service he was employed by the City of Birmingham Corporation Tramways Department, initially as a conductor and later as a motorman (driver).

The Wartime Diary of No.7132 Private William Henry Brooks, infantry man of the 1st Battalion Royal Warwickshire Regiment from August 5, 1914 to November 11, 1918.

The writer of the handwritten diary, William Henry Brooks was decorated with the Victory + , British Star and Clasp. He was 34 years old when the war started. Diaries inherited by John Brooks and on his death, by Heather Boshoff (nee Brooks ).

Hand written diaries transcribed into computer text and edited with Open-Office writer and printed to Adobe Acrobat by Peter Boshoff. Cover design also by Peter Boshoff, using CorelDraw X6. Drawings and illustrations made by Heather Boshoff, who also did the proof reading.

**Acknowledgements.**
**With sincere thanks to** –

Lt Col. Ryan O.B.E. Curator and Mr Brown of the Royal Warwickshire Regimental Museum, for their most valuable assistance and the granting of permission to reprint Official Orders, Narratives of Operations and Special Orders.

The Birmingham Mail for permission to reprint maps and messages from the Front and Official Despatches.

The staff of the History section of the City of Birmingham Public Library for their most willing co-operation.

Research of military documents and newspaper reports of the period by John H. Brooks.

To William Henry Brooks, who's story this is and to his comrades in arms in the trenches during the "Great War for Civilisation" 1914 to 1918.

Picture Credits : Google search : Public Domain WW1 Photo's on Royal British Legion website. (a Percentage of each book after the first 330 books sold will be donated to the British Legion.) Lieutenant Shorter photo's with permission of "www.throughtheireyes2.co.uk."

**Dedication.**

**<u>To his comrades who paid the supreme sacrifice of war :</u>**

Sergeant Major Dodd – Killed in action 1st December 1915
Sergeant Hobbs – Killed in action 17th April 1916
Sergeant Jilks – Missing in action 7th January 1916
Sergeant Law – Killed in action 11th January 1915
Sergeant Williams – Killed in action 21st June 1917
Corporal Hogg – Killed in action 17th April 1916
Corporal Luzack – Killed in action 31st January 1916
L/Corporal Bishop – Killed in action 14th April 1915
L/Corporal Moore – Drowned in action 27th July 1918

**<u>Privates:</u>**

"Taffy" Davies – Missing in action 25th April 1915
"Young" Dunn – Killed in action 25th December 1915
"Tanby" Gibson - Killed in action 11th May 1918
"Ginger" Gold – Killed in action 17th January 1915
"Hed" Hadley – Killed in action 6th September 1915
Jimmy Hawker – Killed in action 7th March 1915
"Dutch" Holland – Killed in action 25th June 1916
Harry Revell – Killed in action 14th January 1916
"Daddy" Watkins – Killed in action 3rd October 1917

**To those whose ultimate fate is unknown :**

Sergeant Major Ganby, wounded 22nd December 1917
Corporal Tynsdale, .......Shell shocked March 1916
L/Corporal Cox, ..........Wounded 19th March 1916
Private "Young" Carter, wounded 1st April 1916
Jack Dark,.................. wounded 7th August 1915,
"Tich" Summers,......... wounded 25th March 1915,
Peter Bishop,
Jack Bull,
"Darky" Burgess,

Bill Cain,
"Barney" Clifford,
"Spud" Heidon,
"Jock",
"Ginger" Kimberley,
"Mac",
Tom Parsons,
"Porky" Preston,
"Scotty",
"Threshy",
Toby,
"Tiddly" Watson,
"Tug" Wilson,

***Appendix 1.***
***British Army Organisation at the onset of the war – 1914.***
***Infantry units***

***Section*** *= 12 to 14 men under Section Commander NCO*

***Platoon*** *= 4 sections under Lieutenant. (48 to 56 men)*

***Company*** *= 4 platoons, plus company officers,1 Major and 1 Captain. (192 - 224 men)*

***Battalion*** *= 4 companies plus 1 machine gun section, plus Headquarters staff – 30 officers, 977 men under a Lieutenant Colonel.*

***Brigade*** *= 4 Battalions plus Headquarters staff. 124 Officers 3,931 men under Brigadier General*

***Division*** *(The major unit of field organisation.) 3 infantry brigades plus 1 cavalry squadron plus 4 field artillery brigades, one of which would have Howitzers and their ammunition columns plus 2 field Companies of Engineers and one Signals company plus 1 Divisional train plus 3 field ambulances.*

***Divisional strength*** *– 5,592 horses, 54 – 18 pounder guns, 18 Howitzers, – 60 pounder guns, 24 machine guns = 585 officers, 17,488 men, under Lieutenant General or a Major Gen.*

***Army Corps*** *2 Divisions plus Headquarters staff, plus extra army troops (Cavalry, Mounted infantry, Horse artillery, Signal units, ambulances etc.) = 40,000 men and officers under a General or Lieutenant General.*

**Foreword by final editor, Peter Boshoff.**
( Opinions Expressed in foreword are the editor's own opinion based on his own know-ledge and insights and information obtained in Wikipedia and sources on internet.)

**The War of the Cousins :** Ever since the times of the Romans, there has been the endeavour of rulers of factions and countries to marry for the sake of alliance. This practice was followed right up to the time of the First World war.

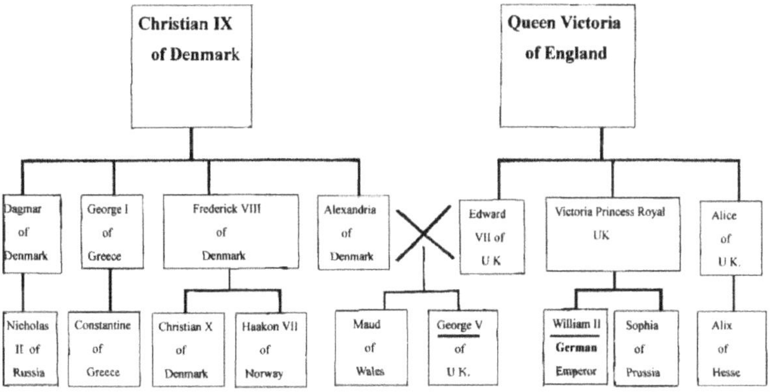


Royal Family Tree.
Queen Victoria's son, Edward VII of England was married to Alexandria of Denmark and their children were Maud of Wales and George V of England.
Queen Victoria's daughter was Victoria Princess Royal. Her son was Kaiser Wilhelm II, (Friederich Wilhelm Viktor Albrecht), born 27/01/1859. He reigned from 15/06/1888 to 9/11/1918. He died 04/06/1941.

George V and Wilhelm II, opponents in the war-time, were therefore first Cousins.

**The causes of the war :**

The true cause of World War I, was the Imperialistic ideals of the German politicians of the time. They did not want to be in the shadow of the British Imperialists. Thus greed for power and domination.

The Serbian government, after the assassination of Franz Ferdinand, heir to the Austro-Hungarian Government, was put in the situation where they could not accept the German ultimatum.

The Germans were ready for war and were only looking for an excuse to start its own expansion. They did not want a World war and thought they could just walk over and invade France and the British colonies on their way to European domination.

England, not wanting their world domination to end or to be subjected to Germany, delivered an ultimatum to the Germans, not to invade Belgium or France. When that was ignored by the Germans, the war started.

The population of Germany was spurred on by newly acquired nationalism.

(Later America was involved due to Germany trying to make an alliance pact with Mexico).

(It took another World war before England sacrificed its own world domination, by giving independence to its colonies. England continued being the "policeman" (due to self-blame of their colonialism and being involved in slavery, centuries before) and still has involvement in conflicts all over the world, right up to the present day!)

**About the book** :

Maps are placed before the occurrence contained in the events of the diary.
Official reports and narratives are placed after the events described in the diary, in italic script.
Photos of examples of the events described in the diary are placed where appropriate.

A glossary of movements, people names and place names is included at the end of the book. The glossary makes use of dates, instead of page numbers.
There is a Table of contents at the beginning of the book after the biography of the author.
The years are used to divide the book in chapters. The months divide it into sub-chapters. (Before the first entry of each month, the year is included, to help keep track of what year it is.)
Photos and Maps are also tabled as a 3rd subheading.

**Biography of the editor.**

Peter Boshoff, the eldest of five sons was born in 1943 and brought up in the Pretoria district, Transvaal, South Africa. After school he attended the South African Air Force Gymnasium. Later he studied medicine and qualified in 1968. In his training he was taught never to rely on second hand knowledge but to investigate and try out everything before committing himself. He became a general medical practitioner, later employed by Anglo American Corporation.
In 1994 he was co-author in a research article on familial non-polyposis cancer of the colon, compiling the family tree of the family involved. This whetted his appetite for writing. Unfortunately work commitments did not allow enough time to start writing until after his retirement.
"The truth is out there, you just have to separate the wheat from the chaff."

# Table of Contents

# CHAPTER ONE...1914

**The start of the war.**

**1914 August**
**August 5th** On receipt of mobilisation papers I travelled to Warwick, to report for duty.
No rations available.
One blanket per man.
Slept on the floor in gymnastic hall.

**August 6th** No entry made

**August 7th** Left Warwick for Newport, Isle of Wright via Portsmouth.

**August 8th** Arrived in Newport at 11am.
Orders at 1pm to go to Freshwater.
No rations until night time.
One blanket between three men.

**August 9th** Parade square drill for four hours.
Daily dinner for two hundred and fifty men served up in a tin bath, which nearly caused a riot.
Plenty of beer but no money to buy it.

**August 10th** Rations served better today, so living fairly well.
Plenty of troop ships in the harbour, ready to move troops.
Allowed out of camp from 4pm until 7.30pm. Had a good concert in the M.E. Tent. There are eighty of us sleeping in it, no room to swear even.

**August 11th** Bathing parade, went down A.1.

A special reserve man shot two fingers off.
Guard duty at night.

**August 12th** Still on guard duty, rained all day.

**August 13th** Squad drill and bathing parade.

**August 14th** C.O. parade on the square. Rained really hard and got drenched.

**August 15th** No church parade.
Went on route march.

**August 16th** Four parades and a medical inspection today. Plenty of grousing from the lads.

**August 17th to 20th** Constant square drill. The squad drill sergeant knows no more about the new drill than we do – a proper "box up".

**August 21st** March to Needles Fort.
Sentry duty at night.
No rations since morning.

**August 22nd** Rations arrived.
Sentry duty at night. Could see twelve searchlights and three lighthouses, sweeping the channel entrance. Naval patrol boats guarding the entrance. No boats or ships allowed to enter the channel from this end.

**August 23rd to 31st** Sentry duty at Needles Fort.

**1914 September**

**September 1st** Route march and trench digging in the morning.
Orders to march to Parkhurst, in the afternoon. A thirteen mile march, in full marching order. Arrived there about 9pm. Nearly all of us are about done in. Almost a riot to get a drink.

**1914 October**

**September 2nd to October 21st** Regular routine.
Medical inspection.
Parades from 7.45am to 1.30pm then 2.30 to 3.30pm. During this time our draft, of two hundred, always paraded under the adjutant - we nicknamed ourselves "the adjutants pets". He told us he would be glad when the blackberries had gone and then he would be able to get some work out of us. We were always told to carry out attacks on the battalion. As a rule we carried out our attacks through a swede or turnip field, then dined well off them. This got us the name of the "fruit draft". We never seemed to do anything right for Colonel.

**October 22nd** Left the 3rd Battalion, about 2.30pm. The Colonel took the Battalion on a route march, so that they would not be in the camp when we left. No farewell from the lads, no band and no good wishes from the Colonel. Oh! : what a send-off.
Arrived at Southampton and finally sailed at about 11pm. The boat is the White Star Line R.M.S CYMRIC

Had plenty of fun loading the horses.

**White Star Line - RMS Cymric. (Same comp. than Titanic )**

**October 23rd** Reached Le Havre, in France.
Splendid weather and the French gave us a good reception.
Marched through the town to the base camp.

**October 24th to 31st** At base camp.

**1914 November**
**November 1st** Left Le Havre for the firing line at Armentiéres.
Spent three and a half days in the train, nine of us in each carriage.
Got out at St. Omer by mistake, then at night we continued in some trucks. Caught the train up late at night and got going again. Got out again next morning and found that we had now come too far.

Marched back to the junction and caught our special train trucks. Got to A.S.C. base, the name of which we did not know and spent the night in a shed.
Plenty of food but I fell over railway wires in the dark and damaged my chin.

***From an Official Report, November 1st 1914.***
*"At the outset of November 1914, the general situation in Western Europe was favourable to the Allies. Every desperate attempt made by the German army to break through to the coast has been frustrated. The British and French artillery had repeatedly proved its superiority thus contributing to the result of the battle; and all along the 260 mile of front from Nieuport to Verdun the Belgium, British and French troops had offered the same firm resistance."*

**November 2nd to 4th** No entry made.

**November 5th** Our section of twelve men sent to hold advanced position – supposed to be very dangerous.
Plenty of shrapnel and snipers.
Three and half inches of water, in the bottom of the trench.

**November 6th** Found a pig which we killed at the farmhouse, in the early hours of the morning, when it was dark.
Jack Bull got shot in the leg at the farm. Swore because he got none of the pig after helping to dress it. Also found some potatoes and made a good meal at night, but got no salt.

**November 7th** No entry made.

**November 8th** Enemy in farmhouse, two hundred yards in front of us. Loopholes all around the farm. Plenty of shelling but still holding the position.
Chum going to the farm to cook remainder of the pig, got shot in the thigh, and unable to move. Crawled along the road on hands and knees and dragged him to the farm. Very lucky not getting hit. Bandaged him up and put him down the cellar, for safety. Stopped with him until dark. They were shelling the farm all afternoon but didn't hit the farm. Took Chum to first aid. He seemed much better.

**November 9th** Getting hotter every day. Gilbert got shot on sentry duty looking through porthole, lucky he was not killed. Relieved Gilbert and they sent another three shots through the porthole but did no damage. We put the sentry in another position. It must have been maxim gunfire. C. Company refused to send relief sentries.

**November 10th** Men getting wounded every day. Wondering who will be next.
Sent message to artillery battery to shell farm, where they had the maxim gun. Artillery fired five shots without hitting it, then the Major said he could not waste any more ammunition. He had "all our best wishes". The enemy set fire to our farm same day.

**November 11th** Terrible night of wind and rain.
Expecting an attack all the time. Enemy attacked about 8.30am. Shellfire very fierce. Lay in pools of water in the road, got drenched to the skin. Continually repulsed the enemy, who finally retired at about 9pm. Not a man hit in the section. Seemed a miracle but what a state we are in.

**November 12th** Fierce shellfire all day.
Cannot move out of bivouac, as snipers are very numerous.
Enemy are trying to shatter our nerves. No casualties.

**November 13th** Section reduced to nine men. Fierce shellfire continues. Using searchlights and rockets at night.
Not getting much food. Haven't seen any stray fowl, lately.
Weather very bad, snow and sleet and cold as charity. Swilled out.
Bivouac falling in.

**November 14th** Terrible weather continues.
Enemy giving us very little rest.
Cannot do any cooking at farm, burnt out completely.
Cannot get reinforcements.

**November 15th** Bad weather continues. All of us wet through and dugout fallen in.
Fierce shellfire. Counted shells for two hours. One hundred and fifty eight shells fired. All shrapnel casualties : three men killed, wounded not known yet.

**November 16th** Still raining and heavy shelling.
Very cold.
One of the company suffocated, caused by dugout falling in.
Killed three fowl. Cooked them in a spare dugout.
Enemy sniping very fierce but managed to cook and eat dinner, without any casualties.

**November 17th** Severe frost in the night.
Toby shot a fowl but it fell the wrong side of the trench. Could not get it till dark.
Free issue of chocolate. Not getting much water.

Under orders to be relieved.

**November 18th** Still peppering away. No luck with any fowl. Enemy very quiet all day.

**November 19th** Plenty of aircraft to be seen.
Enemy shelling again.
Shot three fowl, but unable to cook them, on account of being relieved by the Leinster Regiment. Gave fowl to the Leinsters.(Irish regiment)
Relieved about 8pm.

**November 20th** Marched to Nieppe.
Hot bath and change of under linen. Have been unable to have a wash since leaving the troopship, just a month ago.
Toby killed a suckling pig, and we had a real good feed. Officer sent for Toby and told him to try and find out who stole the pig. Toby said he would try his best. Had a good bit of fun about it. The password is: Who killed the suckling pig?: Ask Toby!

**November 21st** Marched to firing line between Nieppe and Ypres. Relieved the Dublin's. Under inflated fire here. Got about the worst position, as usual. Fairly good cover.

**November 22nd** Snipers very numerous here. Orders to hold position at any cost. Could not show your head above cover without being shot at. Found bodies of both sides, only buried a few inches under the trenches. Everything seems in a terrible state.
Dublins buried a Sergeant in the petty not properly covered over. Also dead body in one of the dugouts. Disgraceful.

**November 23rd** Continues to be very cold.
No bread, tea or sugar issued. This is continually happening.
Made complaint to Officer but did not get any, "coming up later" as usual. No bread issue.
Living rotten. Troops fed up with it.

**November 24th** Rained all night, very cold. The rain has caused dugouts to fall in.
Continual "give and take" fighting. Still holding position. One in company shot fetching water from farmhouse. Not allowed to get any more water from the farm.

**November 25th** Fierce night attack started about 7pm. Enemy repulsed. Another dirty night. Two men of our section were sitting in dugout, eating biscuits and jam, when it fell in. Nearly covered them. Jam pot full of dirt. They did look comical and we nearly split ourselves, laughing. Best laugh we have had since being here.
Plenty of killed men, between the lines, waiting to be buried but we can't get to them yet. Only about a hundred yards separates the two firing lines. We can occasionally hear the enemy singing.

**November 26th** Enemy very active, feigning attacks but we are up to their moves. It keeps us standing to pretty well all night but we get sleep during the day.
Have orders to go to Nieppe tomorrow.
Relieved by the Dublin's at 8pm.

**November 27th** Having a day's rest at Nieppe.
Route march of about seven miles. We look more like tramps than soldiers.

Fresh mutton for dinner and then a good wash and shave. Feeling a lot better after it.
Splendid sleep on straw in a brewery. We got the smell of the beer and that was all.

**November 28th** Still at Nieppe. General clean-up of rifles and equipment.
Boiled beef for dinner but it was spoilt by not having any salt.
Paid out five francs per man - to send out for bread, tea and sugar. Could not get any so we had our money back.
Toby has the backside out of his trousers but they have got none in the stores.
No rum issue, just tea for breakfast. Troops getting very fed up.

**November 29th** Left Nieppe at 3pm, for billeting at farm for the night. Got there at 5pm.
Sections No. 2 and 4 got orders to parade at 6.30pm for trench digging. Marched off in musketry order with picks and shovels, for trench digging. Went to the firing line and started to dig under enemy fire. Finished at 11.30pm.
Dublin's burying a Sergeant close by. Said he got killed when returning from funeral of a private.
Roads up to your ankles in water.

**November 30th** Went for water. Found the rum shop. Had two drinks, got a loaf of brown bread with a canteen of water. On cooking breakfast, I had the misfortune to upset the bacon fat into the water. All my chums laughed until they realised that it was the last of the water. Then they called me everything.
Orders to leave for firing line at 5pm. Relieved Dublin's about 7pm. Roads all under water.
Enemy fairly quiet.

Had orders to strengthen positions. Seems as if we have got to stay here some length of time.

***Official report for the Ypres sector for November 1914.***

*" After further localised skirmishing the 1st battle for Ypres was formally ended on the 22nd of November. This was the last battle in which the German forces attempted a break through to the channel ports. The attempt had been made and had failed."*

*Ypres itself, which was the centre of the bloodshed was in fact a very poor defensive position, far less effective than the high ground around it. The town had unfortunately become a symbol of the fortunes of war and was to be held at all costs. 50,000 British troops had been killed or wounded. The French slightly more.*

*The German casualties are stated at 134,000."*

**1914 December**

**December 1st** Quiet night but plenty of sniping started in the morning. A fellow named Ashford from our section got shot in the head. Done our best for him but he only lived for about half an hour. Buried him at night. Only a simple cross marks his grave. He was his mother's only support.
Went mooching for water at night. Found plenty and some leeks. Lucky no one got hit as enemy sighted us. Pretty warm time getting back and it's raining like the devil. Got reinforcements from home, some of them have only got few months service. They take a lot of looking after, they don't realise that they have to look after their own food. The cold weather makes it harder for them.
Killed stray fowl and shared it between eleven men.

**December 2nd** Both sides of the lines very quiet.
Private Butler slightly wounded in the head.
Weather little warmer and showery.
Rumour that the King is at Nieppe.
Major Arthur Poole re-joined. Been on sick leave with shattered nerves. Never seen him in the trenches. The chaps are joking, that he is sure to get a D.S.O.
Fairly good food last two days. Found potatoes at farmhouse. Toby cooked dinner. Stewed Bully beef, potatoes and yesterday's leeks.

**December 3rd** Enemy very active but no casualties.
The new draft brought a dog out. He got on the top of the trench and got shot before he had been there a minute.
Had a newspaper sent to us, we don't get much news here.

A chap of our company on General Field Court Martial for being drunk and absent three days at Nieppe.
Had some mutton issued, cooked some for breakfast.
One of the new drafts got killed after only being here for two nights.
A Jack Johnson shell burst in No. 2 Section trenches, bursting a spring open. Up to their waists in water and had to send for pump to keep it out.
Big artillery engagement here. Shells all bursting well behind.
Another surprise, butter issued.
Weather very cold again.

**December 4th** Enemy snipers very busy – our loophole riddled. Bullets fell in trench but no-one hit.
Severe storm, hail, rain and wind at about 6pm.
Relieved by Dublins at night.
Marched to farm about three miles away. Roads in terrible condition. Transport having to improve them to move along.
"Nutty" Pinchers got one hundred and sixty eight hours cells, for telling Sergeant Major that he will get the Regiment cut up.

**December 5th** Marched to Nieppe and stayed in brewery to sleep.
Roads in terrible state. Trenches had to be dug to allow the water to run off the roads.
Weather continues very cold and windy and raining.
Had the luck to get some milk for the tea.
Colour Sergeant going home on ten days leave.
Toby marches in without any trousers on causing plenty of fun.

**December 6th** Remain at brewery, got good wash and shave. Issued with clean shirt and guernsey.
Allowed out for one hour. Able to buy some beer but pretty poor stuff – gave it best.
Rained all day.
Met a chap that works on the trams.
Orders to move tomorrow.

**December 7th** Marched to farmhouse for the night.
Rained all day. Got drenched through.
Could not get any bread.
Battalion roll call. Only ninety one men left of one thousand, two hundred that came out with the battalion.
Orders to go in firing line tomorrow.

**December 8th** Still raining.
Inspection of rifles, first aid bandages and emergency rations.
Sergeant threatened to put me under arrest for answering him back.
German shells started bursting all around the farm. We had to clear out of it and stop in a field until it was dark enough to start for the firing line.
All the dugouts fell in. Had to stand ankle deep in water in the trenches. Everybody fed up and wishing for daybreak.
Only biscuits to eat. Went scouting and found potatoes.

**December 9th** Still raining.
We are having a bit of fun shouting back to the Germans. They started to shout "Hurrah" at us. They are barely a hundred yards away, but both sides are strongly entrenched.
Poor rations, no bread again.
Enemy made an attack at night but were repulsed after half hour's fighting.

Private Davis slipped into a Jack Johnson shell-hole, sludge up to his neck. Oh, What a sight! Enough to make a cat laugh. Menu: Bully beef stew.

**December 10th** Rain and very windy. Had to ladle water out of the trench when rain stopped. Started pouring down again before we had barely finished.
No danger of any major attack as all around here is flooded. Big guns cannot be moved.
No bread again and only half rations.
Weather improved at night, but very cold.

**December 11th** Foggy morning.
Toby went reconnoitring and found lots of dead bodies lying in the open, about three hundred yards on our left. Two were recognised as belonging to the Somersets. He returned with German officer's revolver and pebble glasses and some ammunition.
Snipers very busy all day.
Terrible storm started about 6pm lasting all night. Soaking wet and washed out again, with no rum ration till morning.
Germans threw a body out of trench without burying it.
Half rations and no bread again.

**December 12th** Still stormy.
Toby went out again reconnoitring, but got shot in the head. It doesn't seem serious.
Our officer came to tell us that he would like to recommend us for the D.C.M. but could only send one in. We decided on Toby, the Section Commander.
He told us that on average ten thousand shots a day were being fired at our trenches. Still pulling our legs telling us we

are the best section that he ever had. He has sent for his camera so that he can take a snap of us.
Relieved about 7pm.
Marched to farm slept in a barn.

**December 13th** More rain and wind.
Couldn't get any bread anywhere but managed to get some milk.
Orders to move to La Crèche tonight.
Slept in a barn. Had some fun because it was pitch black and we had no light.

**December 14th** Bread, tobacco and chocolate issued today but no sugar for the tea. No wood to make any fires.
Went to village about three miles away, bought two loaves (one currant) for one franc and about two ounces of butter for one franc. Had splendid tea. Currant loaf, butter and jam. The cold tea spoiled it.
The 2nd Mountain Battery of Indians marched through here today. Rough weather and no rum ration.
Made a light with rag and rifle oil.

**December 15th** Cooked breakfast on our jam tin stove.
Battalion issued with fur coats. Our Captain said that we could not have them till the weather gets drier. I expect that we will get them when the weather is dry and warm.
Weather still rough and cold.
Orders to march towards firing line. Slept in a barn about two miles from the trenches. Big guns very busy all night.
Biscuits again, another tooth gone.

**December 16th** Weather improving but very cold.
Busy sharing Toby's parcel of cakes and mince pies. Living fairly well, three and a half loaves each section and what we can plunder.
Large reinforcements of artillery sent here - easily holding the enemy in check.
All that we talk about is Christmas and home.

**December 17th** Sharp frost but otherwise fine.
Germans very busy sniping. They seem to have had more reinforcements with two extra maxim guns. They started to shout "Hurrah", several times in the night, pretending they were making a charge. They do this to draw our fire, to find out where we are, but we have tumbled to their little game.
We made a fire from cabbage leaves, biscuits and a little wood. We did not mind the smell.
Private Davis was telling us one of his yarns ("he's good at it"), until they fired one of their maxim guns. Davis nearly jumped into the fire bucket.
We were telling one of the last draft, what to do if any airships were sighted, he remarked seriously "I don't think they should be allowed to drop bombs on fellows that had only just come out." Rations fairly good, but biscuits again. As I am writing this, there is a terrible artillery duel going on. You can scarce hear yourself shouting.

**December 18th** Weather stormy.
Biscuits again.
Enemy snipers busy. We caught one going to the farm and shot him.
After dark we scouted for water. Just got to the pump when they opened fierce fire on us. Sending up night lights

continuously. We were in a pickle for about a quarter of an hour but luck was with us. No one being hit.
One of the ration party fell into a Jack Johnson shell-hole, full of water and slime. He did look a picture.

**December 19th** Weather stormy.
Orders to stand to and keep up a furious fire, so that the 11th Brigade, who was going to charge some trenches on our right, would not get inflated fire. We were to try and draw the enemy reserves on us. Our artillery keep up a continuous cannonade but unfortunately some of their shells fell near some of our trenches. One of our company was badly wounded. Our officer was swearing like a trooper, and going round like a madman. He had to go sick with a nervous breakdown.
Went out on listening patrol at 5pm. It was a terribly stormy night and we got drenched through to the skin.
Got back to our trenches at 5am. Our trench is like a mill pond and my blanket is soaking wet.
Biscuits again, but what a surprise, butter!

***Official narrative of operations : 1st Battalion R.W. Regiment, 4th division, 19th December 1914.***
*4th division ordered to attack German position to straighten out the line. The 10th Infantry Brigade participated by bursts of fire during the day, while the 11th Brigade attacked in the afternoon. B. Coy on the right with one machine gun fired half right and assisted in the attack. Heavy fire by our own guns all day from which we suffered some casualties. The attack progressed well but actual results not known by nightfall.*

**December 20th** Weather improving, but cold.
Enemy very quiet.
Dried my boots by the fire, but they fell to pieces.

Biscuits again.
Rumour that the Hampshires took some trenches, but our own artillery shelled them. They did not know they had advanced. Nearly two companies killed or wounded. (two companies = four hundred men.) Orders to move out of the trenches tonight.

**December 21st** The artillery gave us bread, cheese and coffee. We had to carry it about three miles. The bag burst but we only lost one round of cheese.
Tea without sugar – no rum ration.
Hailstorm.
Stopped in barn, no lights.
Christmas parcels arrive but we have to leave them till morning.
Another tooth gone!

**December 22nd** Opened our Christmas parcels and all the section shared the puddings, cakes and mince pies. Had a real good time.
Got paid ten francs each. Allowed out for a short time. Got a few drinks of rum and coffee.
Snowed nearly all day.

**December 23rd** Marched to barn near trenches ready to go in tomorrow. Seven of the company absent, four turned up later, drunk. All awaiting General Field Court Martial.
Weather very cold.
Biscuits again.

**1914 December 24th Xmas Eve.**

This is not fiction but God's truth and can be verified by Captain Ernest Hamilton and Lieutenant Cave. We marched to the trenches to relieve the Dublins, at Saint Yvon and arrived at 6am. Not a shot was fired in our direction, which was very unusual. We normally get under fire about one mile this side of the trenches. We really felt a little nervous, as things seemed so out of order.

When we got in the trenches the first thing to happen was hearing a German shouting across "You not snipe, we not snipe, and wishing you a merry Christmas."

Afterwards they started to shout to us, asking some of us to go over to them. After this had been going on for some time we shouted for them to meet us halfway. They consented. One of our fellows went over and a German met him. He took him within a few yards of their lines. They shook hands with him and gave him cigars, and asked him to send over the Officer. One of their men came back with our chap and wanted to be taken prisoner. The officer sent him back to his lines, as he seemed under the influence. Lieutenant Cave went over himself and said not to trust them. However, they had given their word of honour that they would not fire on us, on Christmas day, if we would adhere to the same. The Officer advised us to act as they said and not a shot was fired from either trench that night. I may add they belonged to the 134 Saxon Regiment. We both sent parties out to bury the dead. After that they started singing carols and they also had a band playing. Of course, we all retaliated and all night long it was exchanging greetings and singing. The only thing missing was a drink.

The night was very frosty, a proper Xmas night, but we only had the usual biscuits!.

**December 25th Christmas day.** Not a shot has been fired since yesterday afternoon and we have promised not to fire on them today. We have been walking between the lines, chatting to each other. I had a cigar and a drop of whisky off them. They seem fed up. One of their officers said he would not fire another shot if he had his way. He thought that they had made a mistake in Germany fighting us, but this might be bluff.
They gave us some ham, which we boiled for breakfast. We had tinned army rations for dinner and biscuits yet again with jam for tea.
We had a fire in the trench all day and all night and a Christmas pudding from the Daily News Fund which we shared between ten of us.
It has made us feel so happy and we can scarcely believe it. Seems so out of order. The Germans have told us that they get relieved tonight, so we don't know what tomorrow will bring.

**December 26th Boxing day.** Enemy very quiet and we have been digging trenches all night.
Rained all day and biscuits yet again. We had a debate and came to the conclusion that the Kaiser would have all the Germans "Saxons" shot if he had known what they had asked us to do. Poor devils, they looked done in. They had been told that the German Army had beaten the Russians easily and that they have been in Paris a long time.

**December 27th** Ration party struggled with the rations from about a mile away and then found out that they had lost the biscuits somewhere.
One of the lads upset the Section's rum ration.
Rain tumbling down all night.
Enemy not fired a shot since Christmas Eve.
Got a touch of rheumatics .

**December 28th** Still raining.
Some of the lads went over to the enemy lines giving them some bully beef and jam. The Germans gave them cigars in exchange. They still refuse to fire and say that if we advance they will give in. I for one would not trust them.
The fellows who turned up drunk and late, each got twenty eight days 2nd Field Punishment.
Relieved from trenches.

**December 29th** Wet and cold weather.
Marched to La Crèche.
The Captain told us, that on account of the four men getting drunk, the Company had disgraced itself and he should punish us. We were not allowed out of our billets, not even to buy bread. This is what he calls justice. The troops are getting fed up with it. No rum, half rations of bread.

**December 30th** Marched to Nieppe for a bath and a change of underclothes, then to Steenwerck for inoculation, about fourteen miles away.
Got back at 2am for breakfast.
Warned to mount guard at 5am.
Dry, frosty day.
Half rations of bread.
Boots all in pieces but can't get any replacements.

**December 31st** On guard duty.
Received Princess Mary's Christmas gift.
Orderly man brought some plum pudding to the guardroom. Said it was for the prisoners. After they had eaten it, he found out that it was his Sections' pudding. They chased him out of

the farm. One of the chaps got one hundred and sixty eight hours in the cell for refusing to obey an order.
Rained all day.
Half rations of bread.

# CHAPTER TWO...1915.

**1915 January**

**January 1st** Sent gift home and had to pay one franc carriage. Got boots from the store but no hat. Been without a hat for a month.
Marched ten miles to firing line at Saint Yvon. Rained all the time. Germans very quiet, not a shot fired all night.
Went scouting for wood and potatoes, found plenty.
No bread and still raining.
Lieutenant Cave gave our Section a present each. Nothing off the Captain.

**January 2nd** Showery and a little warmer.
Rumour that we are going for a rest and furlough.
The clean underclothes we had the other day are full of ticks.
Two maxim guns opened fire on us about 6am. What a scamper, some of the company were out on top of the trenches scouting, but no one was hit.
No bread, half ration biscuits.

**January 3rd** Very showery.
Enemy very quiet.
No bread.
Fatigue party carrying boards, for trenches - nearly swam out!.

**January 4th** A German came towards our trench shouting "Good old Warwicks." He took his equipment off, threw it down, put his hand up and gave himself up. He was drunk. They had to put him in a barrow to get him to H.Q.
The enemy have not fired a shot all day.
We can't get much sleep because of the ticks.

Biscuits again.
Still showery.
Have some trouble with my leg.

***<u>From an official observer Report from the front : General H.Q. Jan 4th, 1915</u>*** *"As for the food. No army in the world's history have fed so well as the British army in France and Flanders. Not a grumble was heard during any part of the scattered theatre of operation. With bacon for his breakfast, bread and cheese for his lunches, bread and jam for his tea, and a hot dinner of meat, vegetables and bread. Many soldiers at the front fared better than he did at home and undoubtedly fight all the harder for it afterwards. "Iron" rations consisted of preserved meat, biscuit, tea, sugar and concentrated meat cubes. For the troops in the trenches pea soup was provided twice a week and extra tea and sugar. With luxuries like tinned salmon and coffee from home, so that altogether, Mr Thomas Atkins had little to complain about.*

**January 5th** Had the luck to find plenty of wood. Had splendid fire in the trench. Jimmy Hawker burnt a hole in the bottom of his boots, before he would move away.
My chum Davis seems very bad. I did his sentry duty.
Raining off and on all night. I feel done in.
Orders to move to La Crèche. (Near Nieppe) Got there about 10pm.

**January 6th and 7th.** Paid out ten francs.
Went to the village and had a few ports. It was pitch dark coming back could scarcely see a hand in front of you. I slipped in brook on the side of the road and went in up to my waist. Oh! What a plight! Had to hang all my things up in the barn to dry.

Weather stormy. Country flooded.
Half rations and some bread. No sugar in the tea.

**January 8th** Attended hospital for poisoned leg.
Met young George, reporting sick. He has only been out here seven days. It seems a shame for these young lads: some are specials, some Kitchener's men and some line recruits with five months service . Our battalion has got a mixture now, with only three regular officers left.
Went looking for wood but a machine gun fired at us. No casualties and no wood.
Still cannot get a cap.
Raining and cold.

**January 9th** Orders not to loot farms for wood.
Enemy very active.
Got to farm for wood, crawling on hands and knees in the dark We managed to get some and sneaked off without the Sentry seeing us.
Still holding our position.
Four loaves of bread for each section.
One of the chaps got General Field Court Martial for falling asleep at his post.
Dry weather at last.

**January 10th** Had to go out of the trenches to Hospital, three miles away, to get my poisoned leg dressed.
Had three Scottish Territorial chaps sent to each section for instruction. My sentry chum and I had to go out of the trench to make room for them. We found a room in a farmhouse, for the night.
Biscuits again.
Sunshine all day, rain all night.

**January 11th** Attended hospital, in a café for dressing.
Managed to get a glass of beer.
Sergeant Law shot in the head and killed.
No rum, tea, sugar or bread. Biscuits again.

**January 12th** Relieved out of the trenches 4.30pm. Marched to piggeries.
Three loaves of bread for each section, but no rum.

**January 13th** Engineers fatigue for three hours. Got drenched - back at 4.30pm.
Paraded 5pm for reserve trenches.
On sentry from 6.30pm till 10pm. Trenches full of water - we had to leave them and go in farmhouse. Not enough room to lie down, so we sat up the remainder of the night.
Got back to billets at 6.30am.
Windy and rainy all day.
No rum no bread.

**January 14th** Weather rough.
Rest all day in the piggeries.
Went out for few drinks of beer in the evening. Very poor stuff- nothing like our beer. Could drink a bucket and not know that you had it.

**January 15th** We are still in trouble with the ticks. Itches all over and can't get any sleep.
My chum Davis, with three others, went to Armentieres for the day. Coming back it was pitch dark. The four of them walked into a ditch full of water. We had a bit of fun over it.

German shells bursting around here all day. They blew a house down in Armentieres, killing a young girl about fifteen years old.
No rum or bread.
Living poor.

**January 16th** Orders to move to firing line tonight.
Getting very hot here, shells bursting all around us.
Went to get some water. Some rubbish caught fire as we went along the road, which lit the whole place up. The Germans, seeing us, commenced a rapid machine gun and rifle fire. We had to run for it. The luckiest escape I've ever had. They all agreed that we were not born to be shot.
Enemy very active all night, continually traversing our trench with machine gun fire.
Half rations, no bread.
The trenches are like a river and it's raining.

**January 17th** Ginger Gold got killed with shrapnel. He was waiting to go home, on special furlough, on account of some trouble at home.
Enemy not giving us one minutes rest but they can't get any more forward. One of the worst nights we have had.
Strong north wind, hailstorms and snow.
Half rations, no bread.
Trenches like a river.

**January 18th** Rain and snow, very cold.
The French at Buchy have had to retire leaving some guns, due to flooding. We are all wet through. Everything we possess is wet. Having to keep ladling the water out of the trench, up to your knees in places.

Our officer telling us that we are going for a rest at the end of the month - about time too. Nearly every other company has been, but ours.
Living very poor.
No bread yet again. We have had one and a half rations of bread the last twelve days.
Snipers very busy.

**January 19th** Cold and rain.
Enemy keeping up a very heavy fire.
Our officers are under the impression that the enemy is mining towards our trenches. We are trying our best to find out if it is true.
They made a feint attack at 4am, but we could not draw them too close.
The orderly man fell down a Jack Johnson hole (shell hole) with the bacon. It was full of slime. He was in a state. We have not stopped laughing yet.
Biscuits again and a bucket of pea soup.

**January 20th** Orders to go out of the trenches tonight.
Plenty of sniping.
Left the trenches about 6.30pm and marched to La Crèche.
Raining all the time.
Slept in a barn on wet straw.
Half ration bread and no rum.

**January 21st** Days go as you please, but no use going out as we are only allowed to go within a half mile radius.
Pay out tomorrow.
Half bread ration.

**January 22nd** Marched to Nieppe for a bath and clean under linen.
Paid out ten francs. Went to the village and had a drop of wine.
Cannot buy candles for love nor money.
Weather dry and frosty.
Half rations bread.

**January 23rd** Lance Corporal Handley been awarded twelve months Field Punishment for being absent in France. Another fellow was sentenced to be shot for being asleep on sentry duty, but reduced to three years Field Punishment.
Had a day to do as you please, but only allowed a half mile radius.
Sections No.'s 1,2 and 3 had to pay one franc each, for two pigs and two fowl, that went missing from the farmhouse.
Half bread ration.
Weather dry and frosty.

**January 24th** Went to see the Medical officer, who sent me to hospital, with a touch of fever. The hospital is in schoolroom at Steenwerck. Straw bed on floor but feeling too queer to enjoy the bed. The convalescent patients only get half bread rations here. Have to stay in bed all the time.

**January 25th** Hospital, feeling very queer.

J**anuary 26th** Having no food or sleep. Feeling rotten.

**January 27th** Feeling lot better.
Orderly gave a fellow the temperature tube to put in his mouth. When he took it out, he found out the chap had put the wrong end in his mouth.
Very frosty weather.
No news in here.

**January 28th** Feeling a lot better. Hope to leave tomorrow.

**January 29th** Will not let me leave today.

**January 30th** Still not allowed to leave.

**January 31st** Leave hospital today.
Fellow of the Somersets was shot dead, by a fellow of the East Sussex in an estaminet in Blugh Street. No-one seems to know how it was done. Some say it was an accident and others say it was deliberate.
Wintry weather, snowing.
Half ration bread.

**1915 February**

**February 1st** Heavy shelling in this area. Two R.F.A. men wounded on the road, at our farm.
Go up to the trenches tonight.
Frosty and hailstorms.
Biscuits.

**February 2nd** Made our dugouts into firing trench. Officer told us we should have to make the best of it. Have to sleep sitting up anywhere, in the trench.

Doubled up our sentry duties, doing two hours on and only three off. Stand to from 5.00am to daybreak at 6.45am.
Everybody tired out and fed up.
Rain all day.
Biscuits.

**February 3rd** Filling sandbags all day - enemy snipers busy the whole time.
Report that enemy was seen going into the farmhouse. We sent a party out to attack them, but when they charged the farm, there were only two cats inside. We made plenty of fun out of it.
Biscuits again.

**February 4th** Enemy shelling heavy and three Colour Sergeants hit by shrapnel. Artillery brought aeroplane down in Blugh street. Splendid weather, sunshine all day.

**February 5th** Enemy shelled our position, setting fire to the Headquarters farm and wounding four N.C.O.'s.
One chap shot through the eye in our trench.
Splendid day, sun shining.
We are getting starvation rations - three and a half rations of bread, every eight days.
Relieved from trenches tonight, for La Crèche.

**February 6th** In billets at La Crèche, raining all day but warmer. Enemy shelled and set fire to farm about a mile from here.
Three quarters ration.

**February 7th** Had a bath at Nieppe.
Been paid fifteen francs.
Weather windy and showery.
Three quarters bread ration.

**February 8th** Allowed out. Went and had a look around and a few drinks.
Two of our chaps were found, cut to pieces, on the railway.
Weather rough and rainy.
Three quarters bread ration.

**February 9th** Orders to march to trenches tonight .
A fellow of the Middlesex regiment was shot for being absent from his regiment.
In the trenches, no dugouts. Slept sitting up in the trench.
On sentry duty, six hours out of twelve, at night.
Raining all day. Up to your shoe tops in water.

**February 10th** Snipers busy all day.
Rained all night. Nearly swam out.
Regular biscuit rations issued in the trenches.

**February 11th** Cold but dry.
Tich fell down a shell-hole in the dark and got covered with wet mud. He is that short that we had to make a ladder out of sandbags, so that he could fire from the top of the trench.
Got to hold this position at any cost.

**February 12th** Enemy quiet.
Had to ladle the water out of the trenches.
Biscuits again.

**February 13th** Still raining. Trenches up to our knees in water. Had to get a suction pump to pump it out.
The dugout fell in. This leaves sleeping accommodation for five out of thirteen.
Biscuits again.
Relieved from trenches at 9.30pm.

**February 14th** Got to billets at about 11pm. Had to go on guard duty.
Rough and raining all night.
Three quarters bread ration.

**February 15th** Rain and hailstorms.
Stopped in billets all day and got some milk from the farm, where we are staying.
Three quarters bread ration.

**February 16th** Engineer's fatigue duty, cutting down trees. I think we cut more for ourselves, than for them. We nearly all got a bag of wood chips and had a good fire all night.
Three quarters bread ration.

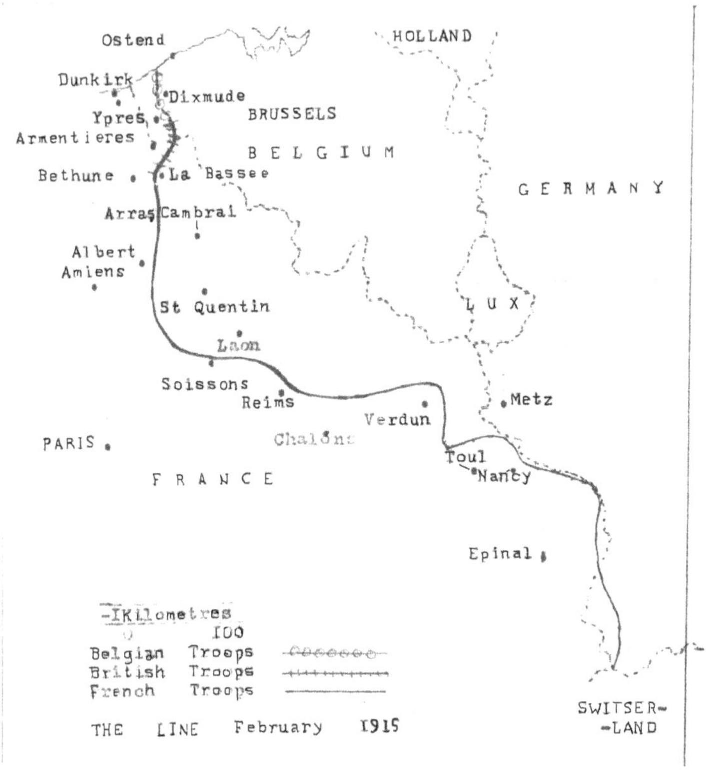


**Map 1 February 1915.**

**February 17th** At long last, being issued with mackintoshes.
Marched to the trenches.
Terrible night of rain and wind.
Half the trench filled up with water and mud, up to your knees in places.
Had to work, all night and day, making new firing positions and getting things shipshape.
No dugout.

Brindley and one of Scottish chaps fell into a shell-hole. Brindley got out, but the "Jock" got stuck and it took two chaps to get him out. He was covered from head to foot in slime.
Biscuits.

**February 18th** Busy digging a new dugout. Every time we throw the dirt out the enemy fires a volley. Private Page got shot through the temple.
Weather fine till night, then showery.
Biscuit rations.

**February 19th** My chum, Davis had a parcel from home and we had a splendid breakfast of bread, butter and pork pie.
The Germans keep throwing hand grenades which fall short but cover us in dirt.
Went on lookout duty in the T-trenches, this is a risky game because you are only fifty yards from the German trenches.
Fine day – biscuits.

**February 20th** Enemy very busy with rifle grenades. One burst near one of our chaps, but the only damage was six holes in his overcoat, not a scratch.
Biscuits and a fine day.
I slipped off the firing parapet and fell into the bottom of the trench, up to my neck in mud.

**February 21st** Relieved from the trenches. Got caught on the way back, for half a mile, by heavy enemy fire so we had to run for it. One of the Dublins got killed.
Misty weather and very cold.
Biscuits again.

**February 22nd** Billeted at a farm in La Crèche.
Full bread rations.
Canadian troops at the camp.

**February 23rd** Marched to Nieppe, for a bath and change of clothing.
Met the Canadian Highlanders, who have just came out from England; they seem a fine set of fellows.
Just heard that another four chaps have been shot for desertion. Full bread rations.

**February 24th** Paid out five francs a man.
Snowed all day.
Paid three francs for a piece of pork, to cook for breakfast.

**February 25th** Got drenched, marching back to the trenches in a rainstorm. Hawker, fell into a ditch on the side of the road, and was soaked to the skin.
Some of the Canadians came with us, for instruction.
Biscuit rations.

**February 26th** Enemy pretty quiet on our front. They made an attack on our left, which was repulsed.
The General remarked that we were holding the most difficult part of the line. He was pleased that we were holding out so well.
Biscuit rations.

**February 27th** Stopped in reserve.
Went on ration carrying and digging from 6am to 1pm.
Had to parade, for firing line, at 1.30pm. We are to relieve the Canadians at St. Yvon. (Two kilometres NNE of Ploegsteert, Ypres area.)

**February 28th** Frosty weather.
Enemy making frequent attacks in the area, but have been repulsed at all points.
We could not get any water today.

**1915 March**
**March 1st** Snow and hailstorms, with a terribly cold wind.
Snipers very quiet.
We have been warned that there have been nine thousand, one hundred and seventy five cases of frostbite at the front, up to date.
Biscuits again.

**March 2nd** Relieved, for fatigue duty, to carry barbed wire stakes to the firing line. Four men wounded on the road.
Three quarters bread ration.

**March 3rd** Fatigue duty from 8am to 2pm, digging trenches close to the firing line. It is very dangerous work, as we are under fire. Very often get someone hit. We are not getting any extra rest out of the trenches, as we are on fatigues all day and part of the night.
The troops are getting fed up.
Full bread rations.

**March 4th** On guard duty at the billets and orderly man.

**March 5th** Marched to the firing line, with some men from the Notts and Derby Regt, who are attached for instruction.

Raining last two days. Nine of the Dublins who relieved us were killed, when one of our own shells fell short. We are now able to tell the types of shell, by the noise it makes in the air.

**March 6th** Rain all day and night. The trenches are like a millpond. We are being worked like niggers and only manage to get three hours of sleep a night.

**March 7th** Plenty of shelling on both sides.
C. Company and the "Jocks" advanced and took some German trenches about 4pm. Jimmy Hawker was shot through the heart during the attack.

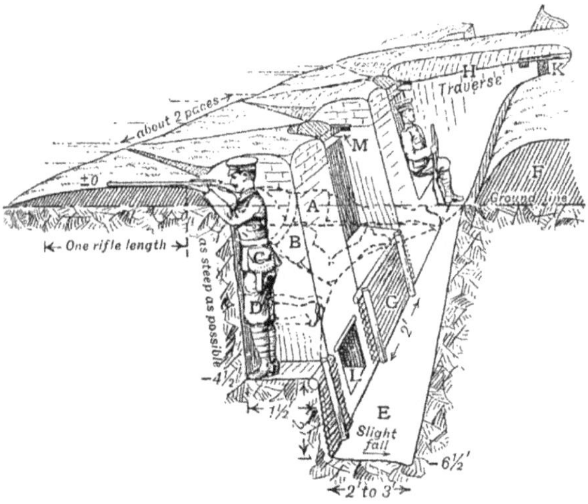


**Illustration 1: Trench construction diagram**

**March 8th** We are getting it very rough. Sentry duty six hours out of eleven, then
digging nearly all day.
We never get any bread rations in the trenches.
All of our section has some sort of rheumatism.

**March 9th** Making a new dugout for my chum Davis and myself. Get relieved out of the trenches tonight to go to a barn, seven miles away, in La Crèche. By the time we got there at 10pm we all felt dead beat.

**March 10th** Confined to the billet, hanging about all day. H.Q. fears an enemy attacks likely, so we are kept at readiness.

**March 11th** Marched to Nieppe for bath and change.
Confined to billet on our return.
Half bread rations.

**March 12th** Confined to billet, ready to move any moment.

**March 13th** March to the trenches tonight. As soon as we got there, we had orders to be ready to move out again by 8pm tomorrow.

**March 14th** Orders for our Brigade to move out of the trenches tonight. Got relieved, marched out and when we were about a mile away, had orders to return to our trenches again.

**March 15th** Orders to be relieved again tonight and then to march to Armentieres.
On baggage guard during the day, then to march, in the evening. We reached our destination about 1am, after getting lost. We were in a pickle and did not know which way to go, but had to trust to luck. We got out all right, as a Staff Officer put us on the right road.

**March 16th** Stayed in a schoolroom but we are not allowed out. No one seems to know our destination. Rations – bully beef and biscuits.

**March 17th** We were inspected by General Sir Horace Smith-Dorrien. We then went back to our old position at La Crèche.

**March 18th** Returned to our old billet, at the farm. We had a good clean up.
Terrible storm started at night. Snow and hail.

**March 19th** Full inspection of arms and equipment and then on engineer fatigues for five hours. We are supposed to be back out of the trenches for a rest, but are messed about so much that we might as well have stayed there.
Snow and hailstorms lasted all day.

**March 20th** Troops getting fed up. We were ordered to do company drill on a ploughed field but had to stop when the Germans started shelling and two of their shells burst two hundred yards away.
Went in reserve at night.
Sixty to a room and not allowed to strike a match.

**March 21st** Ordered to the trenches at Wulverghem.(Messines area.) The enemy is at least five hundred yards away from here, so there is very little sniping, but the shelling is quite heavy. Ordered to man a detached post, for the remainder of the night and returned just before daybreak.

**March 22nd** This is a difficult place to get water or go scouting. The whole place is a mass of shell-holes and movement at night is very awkward.
Managed to find a stream, but have orders not to use it. We just have to disobey these orders and boil it all. There just isn't any more water that we can reach.

**March 23rd** On ration party at night, fell into two shell-holes with the rations and got covered in mud.
Pitch dark and pouring rain.

**March 24th** The enemy are shelling our trenches. Every time we hear a shell coming we had to dive into our dugout. One shell hit a trench and blew one of the chaps right out of his dugout. He was bruised all over and his mac was found in a tree about twelve yards away.

**March 25th** On detached post. Tich Summers was cleaning his rifle, when it went off, blowing the middle of his hand away. The safety catch was locked, but faulty, so he will not get a Field Court Martial for self-inflicted wounds.
Afterwards, Tom Parsons and I were sitting having a chat, when a spent bullet missed me and hit his coat collar, not even marking him. He kept it as a souvenir.
Rained all day.

**March 26th** Enemy quiet.
Relieved in the evening and marched to La Crèche. We got lost again. We were struggling through a ploughed field, falling into ditches and I was wet through. When we got on the right track, we marched, singing "For he is a jolly good fellow". The officer in charge went mad. He knew exactly what we meant, but couldn't do anything about it.

**March 27th** Route march. The boys are fed up. We are supposed to come out of the trenches for a rest. Instead we are ordered on route marches and treated like raw recruits. All you can hear is "Keep in step", "cover off", "hold your heads up". This day has really made us fed up.

Poor rations and we know if we wrote to anyone about it, the censor would tear it up.

**March 28th** Marched to Nieppe for bath and change of underclothes.
Six of the chaps went missing. This is not surprising after yesterday but we are now confined to billets.
Weather very cold.

**March 29th** Our 7th City Battalion marched through here today. The bread is now 8½d for a large loaf. We only managed to get one between us.

**March 30th** In reserve trenches at Steenbecque and went out, trench digging at the firing line from 9pm to 2am. We could see the enemy on the crest of the hill, but our chaps couldn't open fire. We were between them and the Germans and had no cover. Hurt my ankle jumping over a barrier.

**March 31st** Had to make my best way getting back to the reserve trenches, with my damaged ankle - swollen nearly as big as your head. During the day it got much worse. Carried by my chums to first aid post and then sent out to No. 10 Field Hospital.

**1915 April**

**April 1st** Travelled by motor ambulance to Ballyhead. Then by train to the hospital at Bourbourg. The hospital was completely full of wounded and sick, so we were ordered to Rouen.(fifty miles east of Le Havre).

**April 2nd** Arrived at Rouen about 11pm, then transferred by motor ambulance to No. 12 Field Hospital. Had a hot bath and issued with a set of hospital clothes. Splendid bed in Mark E tent. The nursing sisters want to do everything for us.

**April 3rd** In hospital. It seems that my ankle is not broken, but badly strained. Must rest it completely and have dressings.

**April 4th – 22nd** Convalescent.

**April 23rd** Travelled back to base.

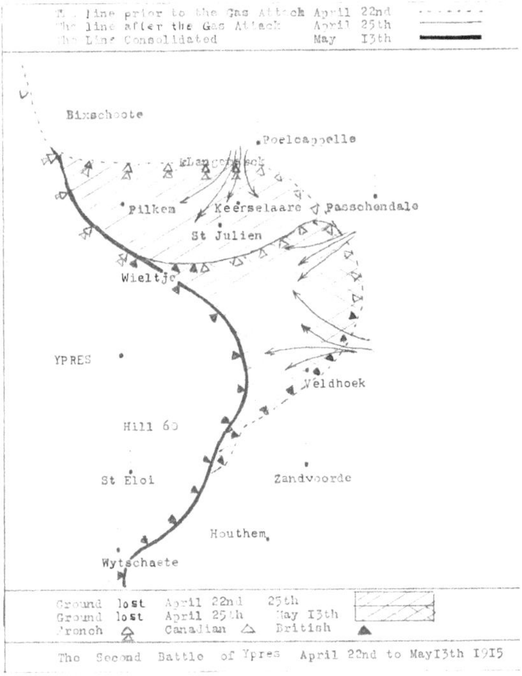


Map 2:Ground gained = ground gained by German army using gas

**MAP 2 May 1915.**

**April 24th** Orderly duty at base.

**April 25th** Sent into section at Ypres.
It was worse than hell itself.
The Battalion was surprised by the enemy, but fought back and advanced right up to the enemy trenches. There were no supports at all, so we had to retire to trenches near the farm at Wieltje.
Orders given "Every man for himself".
The battalion lost between six and seven hundred men and I lost my two best chums. We have only four officers left and there is a large number of wounded, but we just can't get them in.

***Official Narrative of operations : 1st Btn R.W.R.4th Div. 25April 1915.***

*The Brigade attacked at 4.30. We attacked the wood on the left of the line with the 7th Army and Sutherland Highlanders in support. On our right in the attack were the Seaforth Highlanders and the Royal Irish Fusiliers at St. Julien. Owing to the German trenches being insufficiently shelled and support not being able to come up, the line retired at about 7 am to trenches near the farm and consolidated the position. Our casualties were heavy – 17 officers and 500 other rank killed, wounded or missing.*

**April 26th to 30th** In the last five days the battle has raged. The enemy are trying to penetrate our lines but, so far we are managing to hold them.
It's a terrible sight– there are dead bodies everywhere.
We have lost everything except our rifles and equipment.

**1915 May**
**May 1st** We have dug ourselves in but the enemy's artillery has rained shrapnel shells at us all day – it's an awful mess. Terrible conditions and the casualties are horrifying (Forty men today out of two hundred).

**May 2nd** The enemy launched another attack today. These Germans are not human, the brutes are using poisonous shells. Men are lying about everywhere, overcome by the fumes. We tie wet rags over our nose and mouth and try to hold out. It's terrible – if this last much longer we shall soon all be gone. It's really more than humans can stand. Some of the younger ones are praying to die, to get away from it all.

**May 3rd** We had to move out under heavy shrapnel fire, as the whole place is poisoned.
A lot of the fellows have died from the poisonous fumes from the shelling. The enemy is on the attack night and day and most of us now are past caring what happens next.
There are only about forty of us left out of roughly two hundred and fifty – so that seems that in just over a week we have lost a hundred and sixty or more men.
We seem even more determined now, to take revenge on the enemy even if we have to die.

***The second Battle of Ypres : April 1915.***
*The German army launched the first great gas attack at Ypres on the evening of 22nd April, after a heavy artillery bombardment. The North wind suiting the tactics perfectly. Sir John French reports that the poisonous gases were so virulent that our allies , the French, holding the line on the Canadian's left and in the full path of the advancing cloud, were placed horde combat. The Germans followed the cloud and broke*

*through. The Canadians also received a trace of the poison but not so severely. The breakthrough left the Canadian line with a four mile gap at its side and they were in great danger of encirclement. On the 24th the Canadians suffered a second cloud gas attack with many casualties. On the 25th they were relieved by the British under General Sir Horace Smith-Dorrien, who ordered the salient to be kept at all cost.*

**Gas clouds.**

***The official history states :***

*It was presumed that the effects ( of the gas ) would be trivial and local as it had in the past. There were after all Geneva Conventions prohibiting, in spirit at least, the use of such weapons. " The deadliness of the gas lay in its ability to scald and destroy lung tissue. Full recovery, if at all possible, takes a very long time. Protective methods were primitive. Handkerchiefs, wet with water, or more effectively urine, were coated with bicarbonate of soda if it was available. Makeshift respirators were made with lint and tapes for tying on. ( The box respirator was not employed until August 1916. )*

***Sir John French wrote in his dispatch:***

*It proved impossible while under vastly superior artillery fire to dig efficient trenches, or to properly re-organise the line. After the demoralising and confusion caused by the first great gas surprise and the subsequent almost daily gas attacks.*

***Official narrative of operations. 1st Btn. R.W.R. 4th Div. 3rd May 1915***

*Heavily shelled during the morning, Quiet in the afternoon until 4 am, when a cloud of gas was seen catching two regiments in the firing line, which broke. The gas came upon us and some of our men fell back, but we formed up as many as possible and made a line in the rear. The Germans attempted an attack from the wood, which was repulsed with losses. These last three days have somewhat affected the morale of the regiment. A rest from the line is sadly needed.*

**May 4th** Moved back about three miles under big gun fire to reorganise.
We are all suffering from the effects of the poison fumes and feel really weak.
We are all sleeping in an old pigsty.

**May 5th** Standing to all night. Then were joined by a draft of four hundred men, from home.
Things are a bit quieter today.

**May 6th** Went out during the night to dig new trenches. We were under heavy rifle fire, but suffered only a few casualties.
The battle continued during the day.

**May 7th** Digging trenches nearly all night and then the enemy made a desperate attempt to break through. All day the noise was horrible and enough to drive a fellow mad.

**Illustration 3: Trench movements.**

**May 8th** Very heavy shelling all day, which forced us to retire a hundred yards to Potiuze château. Nearly all the trenches have been blown up by the enemy artillery. We estimate about a hundred casualties.

**May 9th** The enemy has almost surrounded us. A section of the East Surrey and some of our chaps have surrendered. We are still trying to keep them back. If we do not get reinforcement soon our number will be up.

**May 10th, 11th, 12th and 13th** The battle has continued over the last four days and we have been going hard, day and night.
I am just overcome with tiredness and fumes.
The enemy has set fire to Ypres.
Relieved by the Cavalry Regiment at night after nineteen days in action.

**May 14th** Moved back and slept in a wood at Vlamertinghe. We have no billet. We got very cold sleeping on the wet ground.

**May 15th** Still in the wood, which is our "official position", while we are waiting for a draft to make us up to strength. Raining most of the time.

**May 16th** Managed to get some rest in the wood, despite the rain.

**May 17th** Ordered to reinforce the 83rd Brigade near Ypres but when we arrived we found that instead of reinforcing them we have to relieve the R.I.F. (Royal Irish Fusiliers) in the firing line. The place is strewn with dead bodies, of every description. The smell is enough to sicken anyone.
We are soaked through by the rain and no dugout to sleep in.

**May 18th** The ration party had a very rough time. They lost half the rations on the way up. Just a few biscuits and some cheese.

**May 19th** They have been trying to shell us out of here all day, but we still hang on. We are working, night and day, to improve our position.
I'm starting to feel quite ill.

**May 20th** Saw the medical officer who sent me to the hospital, suffering from gas poisoning.
The enemy has now poisoned the river.

**May 21st** Arrived at the Bourbourg convalescent hospital.

**May 22nd** Transferred to Bourbourg main hospital and then to hospital at Rouen.

**May 26th and 27th** Moved to Rouen convalescent hospital. Not feeling at all fit yet.

**May 28th** Ordered to base camp at Rouen, where I met my old chum Holland, with a new draft of two hundred, from home. He went home last December, wounded and has come out again.
I'm still not over the gas fumes yet.

**1915 July**
**May 28th to July 8th** On light duty at base camp, while waiting to get really fit again. The rations are reasonable and I am keeping dry.

**July 9th** Re-joined the Battalion near Poperinge.

**July 10th** The whole of the Division is out of the line, for a rest. One of the chaps in the East Surrey's was shot for desertion.

**July 11th to 14th** At rest camp checking rifles and equipment and tidying up, getting shipshape.
Brigade inspection by General Plumer. He congratulated us on our fine work throughout the war and told us that the 10th Brigade, time after time, had saved the situation at Ypres. No one except himself, knew what splendid work had been done during the attacks.

He told us that because of our fine work in the line we were to form the backbone of a newly made corps.

**July 15th to 19th** At rest camp.

**July 20th** Inspection by General French, at Houtkerque. In his speech he thanked the 10th Brigade for saving a desperate situation on April 25th, and many times during the month of May. He said that if the line had not been held it would have been one of the greatest reverses ever suffered by the British army. He realised that we had been without proper cover, for days on end. He said that our nerves must have been under a terrible strain. However, we were one of the bravest brigades out here.
Of course his speech made us all feel very proud.

**July 21st** Orders to move to the line tomorrow, as part of the new army corps.

**July 22nd** Marched ten miles to a railhead and then entrained to Doullens.
From Doullens we marched to Freschevillers, where we slept in the open in the pouring rain.

**July 23rd** Marched another fifteen miles to another part of the line and spent the night in a barn at Bertrancourt.

**July 24th** Inspected by the General in charge of the new Corps.

**July 25th** Relieved the French in the firing line, some distance from a sugar refinery at Sucrerie, near to Mailly-Maillet.

**July 26th** The enemy is very quiet here.
We are very short of water, the ration is half a pint a day.
We are not allowed to light fires so everything we eat is cold.
This is no good.
One loaf of bread between four men.

**July 27th** No entry made.

**July 28th** Enemy very quiet.
Water and rations in short supply.
One loaf of bread between six men today.

**July 29th** Enemy still very quiet.
Water is getting very scarce some days. It is about a four hour journey away, at the refinery where it is issued with the rations.
Rations are still very poor.

**July 30th and 31st** One and half loaves, to this section of eleven men.

**1915 August**

**August 1st** The enemy artillery has been quite active. We have suffered some periods of shellfire.
Rained nearly all day and we are soaked through.

**August 2nd** On ration party. Had to go on a three hour journey to fetch the tea and got caught in a violent storm. The tea was cold, when we got back and no fires to warm it up.
There are no dugouts, to shelter from the rain.
We can't find any wood from which to make a fire.
We are wringing wet through and no warm food.
The enemy are making saps.(Covered trench)

**August 3rd** The trench is in a terrible state, through the rain.
Up to our knees in water and mud.
The enemy are shelling hard.
We have made an official complaint about the rations.

**Up to our knees in mud.**

**August 4th** Enemy shelling and sniping at night.
We had currants and sultanas today instead of our jam ration.
On sentry duty. We have had to find four sentries out of five men. I have done seventeen hours on duty, out of twenty four.
We are just worn out.

**August 5th** Plenty of sniping and shelling. Rations still poor.

**August 6th** A party of the enemy advanced down one of their saps, to wait for our man to go out to the listening post. We spotted them and they cannot get back.

**August 7th** A grenade party was laid on to capture the enemy. My chum Jack Dark got shot in the wrist by one of our own men on sentry duty, further up the line, who didn't know about the scheme. Jack carried on with the others, then they realised that there were too many of them to attempt a capture. They lobbed in the grenades and managed to crawl back.
Jack has been recommended for the D.C.M.

**August 8th** Enemy bombarding us with aerial torpedoes but have done very little damage with them.
Orders to be relieved tonight.
Not had a wash since July 25th .

**August 9th** Relieved at night and marched about twelve miles to a billet at Lealvillers, arriving at 4.30am.
Orders have come through that I am to be attached to the Regimental Police.
Change of underclothes and a bath.

**August 10th to 14th** In billets at the farm, resting and spinning yarns.
Sleeping and eating quite well.
Drilling in Acheaux Park.

**August 15th to 21st** Marched to Mailly-Maillet.
Spent four days and nights, in shifts, digging reserve trenches.
Some at night, some at day - four hours on, eight hours off.

**August 22nd** Watched an aeroplane duel, the result of which seemed a draw.
All leave cancelled.
Orders to move to firing line.

**August 23rd** Marched to firing line at Sucrerie.
Conditions much better, managing to build dugouts with wood brought back.
Rations improved.

**August 24th** Enemy very quiet – just a few trench mortars and aerial torpedoes.
No casualties, full rations.

**August 25th** Enemy still very quiet. We are improving our position with good dugouts.

**August 26th** Enemy very quiet – just mortar and torpedo fire. The Territorial Battalion on our left, fired off twelve mortars but only three of them went off. The enemy retaliated and we had six men killed and twenty six wounded.
Orders to be relieved tonight.

**August 27th** Marched to a billet, in a barn, but got very little sleep because of strange noises.
We thought that the place must be haunted. We lit a candle and saw bats flying about all over the place.
We had some fun but very little sleep.

**August 28th** On parade for a farewell speech by Colonel Poole. He thanked us for all our good work, which had resulted in him being promoted to Brigadier General. He said that he was very sorry, that he had been forced to be a very hard task master.
He felt it had been necessary for the Regiment and the British army.

**August 29th and 30th** In billets in the barn.
Rations quite good and plenty of water.

**1915 September**
**September 1st** Marched to the firing line.

**September 2nd** The enemy are active, lots of sniping and trench mortars. We had a hand-grenade duel during the afternoon. Weather bad.

**September 3rd** Enemy still active with aerial torpedoes and sniping.
Not allowed any fires. All our food and drink are cold.

**September 4th and 5th** Again no fires, still under grenade and mortar fire.

**September 6th** Germans very barbaric. I lost my old chum Hadley who was killed by a sniper.
Not any fires allowed again, so all our food is cold.

**September 7th** Enemy still active and it is getting very rough here with sniping, grenades and aerial torpedoes.

**September 8th** Orders came through for leave but I was told later that none of the men that had been in hospital, through gas were allowed leave – rotten luck.

**September 9th** To be relieved tonight. Having hand-grenade and trench mortar duels. They are getting barbaric here.

**September 10th** We were relieved and marched to billets at Varennes.

**September 11th to 14th** Had a good rest.
Rations quite good.
Bath and change of underclothes.

**September 15th** Marched to the firing line at Sucrerie

**September 16th** Enemy very active, it's getting hot here. Lieutenant Cooper was wounded and died in the night, on his way to hospital.

**September 17th** Sprained my ankle and given twenty four hours excused duty. Spent the time in the dugout getting things shipshape, and reading a book. The rations are coming through much better and we have some water.

**September 18th and 19th** No entry made.

**September 20th** Enemy not so active over the last two days. The weather has been reasonable.

**September 21st** No entry made.

**September 22nd** Orders to be relieved tonight. Enemy much more active. Heavy shelling, grenade and mortar duels.
It is surprising how light our casualties have been.
All leave has been cancelled again, so something big must be coming up.

**September 23rd** Marched to relief billet, at Acheux, for a wash, change of underclothing and a good rest.

**September 24th** Orders to move out and prepare for some serious fighting, as a big advance is expected.

**September 25th** The 1st Army is advancing and progressing favourably. The French are also on the move, doing some good work. Unfortunately, it is raining hard again which may bog them down.

**September 26th to 28th** Moved out and took up billets at Beauval, sleeping in hammocks suspended from the ceiling.
On the first night one of the chaps wired them together and around midnight started to swing them violently.
We all suspect "Porky" but can't prove a thing. Anyway we had a good laugh over it.
Weather still very bad and we are standing by.

**September 29th** Marched to the firing line at Sucrerie, preparing for the advance, but terrible weather, so the advance is cancelled due to the bad state of ground.
It is impossible to move the big guns.

**September 30th** Enemy active and sniping and plenty of mortar attacks.

**1915 October**

**October 1st to 4th** Enemy very quiet again.
We are living quite well, despite there being plenty of mud everywhere.
Luckily, the rations are coming through.

**October 5th** Enemy active with sniping and mortar fire.

An enemy spy was caught in the firing line, dressed as a British Captain. We have had a full roll call and are searching every nook and corner in the trenches for any more spies.

**October 6th** To be relieved tonight.
There was an aeroplane duel right over our heads. The enemy was forced down just behind our lines. A party was sent out to take them prisoner. They found both the pilot and observer shot dead.

**October 7th** Marched back to relief billet.

**October 8th** Had the usual bath and change of underclothes and our swing in the hammocks.

**October 9th to 12th** Stayed in billets, had a good clean up of equipment and a good rest at night.

**October 13th** Marched back to the trenches, taking some of the Dublins with us. They are Carson's army chaps and we are breaking them in.
It is fairly quiet.

**October 14th** Very misty this last two nights.
The Germans have erected a notice board on the barbed wire and it reads "You have done well at Loos and La Bassee, what are you going to do here?" I bet they would like to know.

**October 15th** A patrol of Royal Irish met an enemy patrol, which hastily made off. The Irish investigated what they thought was a German left behind. It turned out to be a

dummy. While they were messing about with the dummy, some Germans got behind them.
The Irish managed to escape but two of them got wounded.

**October 16th and 17th** Enemy very quiet.
Working on the trench and the dugout to "improve our living conditions".
I bet that as soon we have it really shipshape we shall be moved.

**October 18th** A terrific artillery bombardment started up at 3am. It was a very hot three hours while it lasted.
We were very lucky to have only twelve men wounded.

**October 19th** Enemy very quiet again today.

**October 20th** One of the chaps in D. Company, on sentry duty, heard someone drop in the parapet at 1am. He went to find out who it was in the dark and ran straight into a German. He was too close to use his rifle or bayonet, so he closed with him and tried to trip him.
The German had a revolver and put five bullets in the sentry. He shouted to him to stop but the German ran into another trench, met another fellow getting out of his dugout and shot him dead. A second chap, getting out of his dugout was stabbed with a dagger.
The curious fact about it is that he got clear away.
Patrols searched everywhere but he is still at large.
I think he got back to his lines.

**October 21st to24th** Enemy quiet.
Living fairly well.
Relieved and marched to our hammock billet.

We had a good clean up all round and a rest.
Orders to move off to Acheux.

**October 25th** Inspected by the King in the pouring rain.
I might mention he looked far more worried than any other man on parade.

**October 26th to 28th** Moved back to the billet and had a quiet time.

**October 29th** Marched back to the firing line.
The King's Own have had very heavy casualties - Forty eight in the trenches.
Very dirty weather.

**1915 November**
**October 30th to November 3rd** Raining consistently, the whole time.
Nearly all the parapets are falling down and the water is over your shoe tops everywhere. We are spending the whole time trying to keep some sort of order.
Two men in the company were killed when the dugout fell in on them.
We are all wringing wet through.
Having difficulty getting the rations through.

**November 4th and 5th** Still raining and the trenches are falling in everywhere.
Up to your neck in mud.
On short rations owing to them getting lost.

**November 6th** Weather turned out foggy at night but dry and cold during the day.

**November 7th** One of the blokes brought an aerial torpedo into the trench, which had failed to explode. It was to be sent back for examination but it exploded and blew five of them to bits.

**November 8th** A strange thing occurred in reference to yesterday.
The Sergeant Major gave one of the fellows a novel the same morning, entitled "The Fatal Five".

**November 9th** Told to get ready for leave, starting from here on Friday morning at 2.30am.

(**1915 Notes on my turn of duty over here.**)
The Belgian dogs do a great deal of work which surprised us. They are harnessed to carts, like little horses and work treadmills at the farms.
Nearly all the large buildings, including the churches are in ruins. The damage in Belgium is far worse than in France.
We met hundreds of Belgian refugees at Calais, living in railways buildings and sidings. Some of them are a pitiful sight and they don't really seem to care for the French.
Nearly all the bridges that we passed have been blown up at some time since the war started.
Met an Indian contingent at St. Omer, a fine body of men, who gave us a very good reception.
There is much amusement here by a newspaper article on the Army Service Corps in the trenches. We have never seen one of them nearer than two miles. We reckon that this chap must have got lost.
We are all concerned by the arrangements for the wounded. Our own stretcher bearers carry them for at least two miles before they reach the post where the R.A.M.C. take over. We are trained in first-aid but that is all.
The Belgian people are really great, they just give you anything that they have and just cannot do enough for you. Poor devils, their land is poisoned and will remain so for years.
We now realise that it is the poisoned land that give us so much trouble with our wounds.
The French are not at all like the Belgians – they are always trying to beg off us and give us nothing.
The church clock at Armentieres strikes the half-hour just the same as the hour.
We are warned that that the Germans are now using a lot of explosive bullets in the area of Nieppe.

**November 21st and 22nd** Travelled back off leave.
Thousands of people in London to see the leave men off to France. One of them even joined the train and played his violin to cheer us all up.
We all seem tired out on the boat, but it was a smooth crossing. After sixteen hours in the train we reached Acheux, too late to get a drink.

**November23rd** In billets in a barn swarming with rats.
The weather is terrible, snowing and very cold.

**November 24th** Still in billet.
Peter Bishop has tied his money up in his handkerchief ,as he is convinced that the rats are taking some of it away.

**November 25th** Marched to the firing line near Mailly-Maillet.
It is very cold, freezing all night and day, making it difficult to get water.

**November 26th** Enemy very quiet.
They have put out a notice none of us can understand. Even the officers cannot decipher it. The notice says : "The Kaiser and the Jills, the 29th of the month".
Carson's army in this position for the first time, got all in a state when they thought they were in a path of a cloud of gas. They all put their gas helmets on and started running about. One poor chap nearly suffocated. Plenty of leg pulling going on over this.

**November 27th** Still fairly quiet but it is freezing hard. We have some frostbite cases and a lot of chaps are suffering from sickness.

**November 28th** Still fairly quiet but very cold and a lot of sickness.
Casualties very light.
Rations fairly good.

**November 29th** Enemy quiet.
Weather very much warmer and it has started raining.

**November 30th** Rained all day and night – the trenches are in a terrible condition.
Conner was out, as a guide to a working party, when he fell into a hole full of water. The officer in charge fell in on top of him and gave him a real dressing down. Conners did manage to tell him that he didn't do that sort of thing for the fun of it!
One of the R.E. horses fell into a trench and it took four hours to get him out. Apart from being shaken up he seemed very well. Thirteen of our air planes passed over here, they must have been on a raid somewhere.
Poor rations, half a loaf of bread between four men.

**1915 December**

**December 1st** Weather very good during the night, but very dark.
Our artillery bombarded the Germans this afternoon. They blew up some of their dugouts and we opened fire as they ran out. They must have suffered heavily.
One of the "Jocks" drowned, falling in a big hole full of water.
Sergeant Major Dodd was killed by one of our sentries. It seemed that the Sgt. Major went out on the top because the trench was full of water. The sentry challenged him but had no reply, so opened fire. On sentry duty you have orders to shoot at anyone fails to respond to the challenge.

**December 2nd** Rained nearly all day.
An orderly from D. Company got stuck in the mud. They pulled him out but left his jack boots buried in the mud.

**December 3rd** Orders to be relieved by the 10th R.I.R. Carson's Army. A lot of them seems to be frightened to death.

**December 4th** Marched to relief billet at Forceville.
Everyone is plastered with mud and wet through.
One hundred and twenty went sick this morning, some of them went wrapped in blankets because their clothes were all wet through.
Our Regiment played the Seaforth Highlanders at football and beat them 2-0. Plenty of excitement.

**December 5th** Went for a bath, but after we had dis-robed there was no soap and no change of underclothes. Put our wet clothing back on again.
Put a drunken Frenchman in the stable, and locked him in, to sleep it off.

**December 6th** Resting in billet, still wet but much warmer.

**December 7th** Walked about five miles to watch the Regiment play the Dublins at football. It was an exciting match which the Regiment won
3 – 0, but it poured with rain and we are soaked yet again.
Orders to the firing line tonight.

**December 8th** Marched to the trenches. The mud and water making things very difficult. The communication trenches are waist high in water, so we had to go over the top.

Our own trench is in a terrible state, but we have been issued with waders.
I fell in a soak hole in the dark. I was up to my neck in water, but managed to get out.

**December 9th** No entry made.

**December 10th** It is getting past a joke now.
It is still raining and you have to wade through water up to your waist. The enemy snipers are very alert, so we can't chance going on top to get out of it.
We are under heavy shellfire during the day but no one was hit.
Some of the working party got stuck in the mud and had to be roped out, but they left their boots behind.
Visited by the General.

**December 11th** Snow and rain.
Corporal Whitehouse fell in a soak hole during the night. One of the chaps passing in the morning found him, and managed to drag him out. He is really queer though, suffering from exposure.
Still up to our waists in water.

**December 12th** Frosty dark night.
Some of the stretcher bearers taking a fellow to be buried, had to go over the top as the trench was in such a bad state. They put the stretcher down to escort a sick chap to see the doctor. When they came back they could not find the place where they had left the body. It is now midnight and they are still looking for it.
News has just come through that "Lady" Hill had to escort the General to the "Jock" lines. He got stuck in the mud and the General had to pull him out.

**December 13th** They found the stretcher early this morning. Getting relieved tonight.
Leaving the trenches I met a fellow of the R.I.R. on the ground. I went to his assistance, thinking he was wounded. Instead I found he was drunk, and left him.

**December 14th** Raining again and very cold.
Got to the relief billet at Colincamps.
The Sergeant Major gave us an order to have our hair cut short. We refuse to "look like convicts" . I don't know what will happen over this.

**December 15th** Raining and very cold.
Full rations – living quite well.

**December 16th** Corporal Tynsdale was due for Field General Court Marshal today for being absent for five days without leave, but owing to the Court Martial papers not being sent in time to the Brigade office our own C.O. just gave him a severe reprimand. Went to see our Regiment play the Argyll's at football but we lost 4-0.

**December 17th** Ordered to go in the trenches tonight.
It was pouring with rain and we got wet through.
It has been very quiet all night, some of the Carson's Army, next to us are a poor lot, griping all the time. They have only been out here five weeks.
I met Pitcock of the Rifle Brigade, but could not stop for a quiet chat.

**December 18th and 19th** Weather fair.
We had some of the chaps from the South Lancs, joined us, for instruction in trench work. They had a bit of bad luck, one killed and two wounded before they had been here many minutes.

**December 20th** Bright moonlight night.
The South Lancs went out, with our chaps, on a working-party. They came under fire and suffered one killed and one wounded. They had to leave the body, in a backyard till morning, as they had no burial party. As I was on sentry duty, I had to keep visiting it, to keep the rats away.

**December 21st** Heavy artillery on both sides, still raining.
We had an issue of fresh meat, which Peter took over to make us some grilled steaks. He said it was a treat but it tasted like burned toffee.
Received my Christmas parcel from home and had a great time sharing it out with a few of my chums.
Orders to be relieved tonight

**December 22nd** In a barn at Varennes. Ginger Kimberley led us on a short cut. We got stuck in the mud in a ploughed field and nearly lost our boots.
Had our bath and change.

**December 23rd** Went to Varennes and had a great night in the estaminet, (Wine shop) plenty of wine and a sing song. Some of the gunners tried to open a window but pushed it the wrong way and smashed it. It cost fifteen francs for the damage.

**December 24th** Rainstorms again.
A chap of the R.A.M.C. stole a goose from the farmyard and got twenty eight days Field Punishment.
We sat up until about 1am drinking French wine and having a sing song.

**December 25th** We moved to the trenches today. We started at 3.45pm.
I have received another parcel from home and living well.
Breakfast : cake and jam, Dinner : cake and bully beef rations, Tea : bread, butter and a little sliced tongue. Tea without milk.
Our issue of rum was stolen.
Very dark night and raining.
Slipped into a shell-hole, got very muddy and slightly sprained my wrist.
Private Dunn, was killed by a sniper, the first time he had been to the trenches for five months. He had been back at base on boot repairing duty, because they found out that he was a cobbler in civvy street.
Threshy gave a great big tin of cocoa away that was in a parcel from home. Bill Cain, opened it today and found a bottle of whisky, packed round with shavings inside. What will Threshy say when he finds out!
I am awake to see Christmas day out as I on sentry duty, 11pm till 1am.
It is raining like the devil.

**December 26th** Very stormy.
Someone sent Spud Heidon a white waistcoat. It's a proper ancient one. We've been kidding him that it is the one his grandfather got married in. We had him proper wild. Spud got married when he was on leave and hasn't been the same since.

It was up to me to fetch the water tonight. I had to go about a mile and a half over ploughed fields. You could hardly see your hand in front of you, it was that dark. I was in a mess and kept stumbling into shell-holes and losing the track. It took me two hours to cover the mile and a half.

**December 27th** Fierce artillery bombardment on both sides but very little damage done.
We are overrun with rats. You can't get to sleep without covering your head over, very trying.
The nights are pitch black.

**December 28th** The first fine day for weeks.
There has been a lot of aircraft about all day. Neither side could claim a victory. It has been a treat to watch their duels.
Plenty of artillery and sniping on both sides.

**December 29th** Very fierce enemy bombardment, which ploughed the ground up all around us. Very few casualties.
We are to go out of the trenches tonight.

**December 30th** Vile weather. It has been raining on and off this last week.
We billeted at Acheux. Had a bath and change of underclothing.
Private Brown was caught near Paris. This is his third time of desertion. Looks like he will get shot.

**December 31st** Our Company played the "Jocks" at football. The "Jocks" won 1-0. It rained all the match and we all got soaked. Captain Irvine gave a dinner and smoking concert for the company. It was a splendid turn out, just like being at home again, seeing the table laid. We had almost forgotten how to use a knife and fork.

# CHAPTER THREE...1916

**1916 January**

**January 1st** Orders to move to Mailly-Maillet, which will be very close to the firing line. We all are expecting something big to come off.

I think we are in a house, half the roof is off, and there are no windows or doors. It's worse than being in the open. The French have been in these billets. They are in a stinking dirty state. They have been too idle to go out the back to do their business.

**January 2nd** Raining all day.

We have to go digging, up in the firing line every night. It is in a terrible state, like a river.

**January 3rd and 4th** Enemy very active with artillery, but doing very little damage.

One of their aeroplanes dropped bombs near to our No. 2 Company on relief, at Colincamps but no damage done.

Orders to move to the east of Les Boeufs.

**January 5th** We will be going into the trenches tonight.

Orders to keep under cover, as our own artillery are bombarding the enemy trenches.

Rations poor, no vegetables.

**January 6th** Artillery duels all day. The enemy have blown away part of our parapet. We were lucky to have only one killed and two wounded.

**January 7th** Reconnoitring party to the salient ready for our expected attack. The party came under fire and had to run for it. Sergeant Jilks was hit and his body has not been found. They heard him say "God help me, I'm done for". We surmise the Germans took his body in. We do not know whether he is alive. Rations still poor.

**January 8th** There were orders to take the salient tonight but it got cancelled. I expected that the officers are worried in case they got information from Sgt. Jilks, when they searched him. There has been heavy shelling today, but our batteries have been giving three for one of theirs.
An Officer of the Dublins got wounded. He was out on patrol but failed to answer the sentry when challenged.

**January 9th**. Weather bucking up a bit.
They have been shelling us heavily today, but we have few casualties.
Brigadier General Hull went out with one of our patrols, last night. We think he is one of the bravest Generals out here. He always has a cheery word for everyone.
Relieved at night by the Irish Fusiliers.

**January 10th,11th,12th** Billeted at Forceville.
There was an inspection of all arms and a general clean up. Getting very poor rations here, have not had any kind of vegetables for a fortnight.

**January 13th** Marched to the trenches but did not have a single casualty getting in which is most unusual.
Ginger Kimberley has got hold of a rat trap. We have caught two very big ones (one was running off with the trap).
The Germans are very quiet.

**January 14th** Artillery duels and plenty of aircraft about all day. Harry Revel was killed going on patrol, by the German salient.
I'm smoking a nice cigar which Ginger gave me. He is on sentry duty.
No luck with the rat trap today.

**January 15th** Enemy fairly quiet. At about 3.30am, two Prussians of the 180 Regiment were caught inside our barbed wire. They were shot dead by the sentries. Each of them carried six bombs and a loaded rifle. They were poorly clad, both of them wearing two pairs of trousers. We think that they had been sent to destroy our machine gun post, which has been giving them a lot of trouble.
A draft of thirty eight joined us from home.
Ratting : Two more today, one dead and one escaped, wounded.

**January 16th** Enemy very quiet and the trench is drying out well.
Our waders are good in the deep water but we slip and slide everywhere in the mud. Plenty of fun with chaps falling in the mud.
Four men wounded tonight, all within five minutes.

**January 17th** Bright morning.
At about 11am we counted thirty two of our aeroplane coming back from a raid on the enemy lines. One of them came very low over the enemy lines, was subject to heavy rifle and machine gun fire but seemed to be unhurt. We think that he did it on purpose to find out the enemy's strength.
Orders to be relieved tonight.

**January 18th** New billets at Colincamps which is only about one and a half miles from the firing line. Plenty of enemy shelling here.
You never know when you are going to get your billet knocked down.
Bath and change of underclothes.

**January 19th** Fairly good weather again.
Private Mason got three months No.1 Field Punishment for being absent. He just refuses to do it and sits down. They have sent him to Divisional H.Q. and we reckon that he will get about two years.

**January 20th** Managed to get a football today and have had a great time playing football between ourselves.

**January 21st** Still at Colincamps.
A lot of our chaps were ordered to go trench digging, up at the firing line. It was bright moonlight and they refused to go out on top. Fourteen of them have got field punishment, but at least they are alive.
Spud bought two eggs for sixpence, one was rotten and the other went green when he cooked it. He is going mad and threatens to kill all the French as a reprisal.
Ordered back to the firing line tonight.

**January 22nd** On guard over the water supply.
Lieutenant Spencer was killed by a sniper, as he was out testing the German barbed wire, last night.
There has been one of the heaviest artillery bombardment on both sides – about the heaviest we have had on this part of the line. Trenches are smashed in on both sides as shells are dropping all around. Lieutenant Sharp, was our only casualty. He had the muscle in his arm blown off.
Our own artillery forced some of the enemy to leave their trenches, then our machine gunners bowled them over.
We had to leave our "fire bucket breakfast", as the shelling was so hot.
Spud dodged off somewhere as he suffers with his nerves in heavy shelling but always turns up when it eases again.
They have blown up some parts of our miniature supply railway line.
Ginger had to fetch the rations from about two miles away. When he got back he had the wrong bag. Someone had to go back, so I went in the pitch dark.

**January 23rd** Very misty.
Plenty of sniping all day. They have been shelling us on and off all day. One shell dropped within ten feet of where we were standing, but no one was hurt. It seemed a miracle.
Poor Spud is going about like a man in a dream. He doesn't know what to do with himself, his nerves are fairly shattered.

**January 24th** Fairly quiet all day but the Germans started heavy shelling at night.
Our front line working party, of a hundred and fifty strong, came under fifty rounds of rapid fire. Not one man was hit. Pure luck, everyone said.

We went out scouting for wood. All we could find was part of some farm machinery. We had to smash it up to get the wood off. It seems a sin, but we have to get fuel somehow.
Rain and drizzle all day.

**January 25th** Fairy quiet today. On digging party at night, making a new trench. We keep turning up dead Frenchmen. It smells really terrible but we must stick it out.
Orders to be relieved tonight.

**January 26th** Marched back to our relief billet at Forceville. Got a bath and change of underclothes.

**January 27th** We have orders to be much tougher with our own prisoners. On top of their daily work, they must now do two hours pack drill and be tied up for an hour.

**January 28th** It seems as if we are soon going to leave this part of the line, as the Quartermaster is issuing plenty of new clothes. Every man has got a new shirt, a pair of socks and any uniform needed.
My chum Porky and I went on a pass to Acheux. We went to see a pantomime, it was very good. We bought a couple of oranges to make it seem more real. We were cautious around the sentry, as he shot at some of our fellows last night. (They had bustled past him without a pass). He has had his leg pulled all day because they were only fifty yards away and he missed them.

**January 29th** Went to the trenches about 5.30pm.
The enemy started shelling very heavily, as we were going in, but no one was hit.

Poor Spud was nearly dead with fright. He kept on shouting "Brooky, I'm nearly done in and will fall down in a minute". I think he will soon go balmy. He is as nervous as a kitten now and all the boys are pulling his leg.

**January 30th** We have not got a very pleasant job, as we have to go over the top to get to our lookout posts. The snipers are always trying to pick us off. It has been misty, this last few days so it's been in our favour.
We are sweating about getting attacked by gas. They have used it on both our flanks and we expect it must be our turn next.

**January 31st** Corporal Luzack got hit by an enemy sniper near No. 9 post. For some reason he was out on the top. We had to dig a trench towards him to get him in, but found he was already dead.
Just received a message from H.Q. to warn us that the chaps at Curzac, to our left, are being subjected to gas attacks. We have to keep in readiness, in case it reaches us.
There has been a terrific bombardment, on our right.
It has been a very misty day again. It causes a lot of trying work.

**1916 February**
**February 1st** The enemy are fairly quiet.
Special orders to be relieved, then move down country for a rest period.
It's a beautiful day but very cold.

**February 2nd** We left the trenches at 6.30pm.
Went into billets at Colincamps for two days.

**February 3rd** Orders to parade, in full marching order, at 9.30am to proceed to Montcourt for a rest.
Marched in full order and arrived at 1.30pm.
We are billeted in the harness room of a very big châteaux.
The people here are more obliging than any we have been with before.

**February 4th,5th,6th,7th** We are doing military training about six hours a day.
A draft of about fifty joined us, from home.
On the 5th, they caught young Brown. He had got away from an escort some two months back. This is his third time of desertion. He was in our charge today, for the purpose of identification. An escort collected him about 2pm. I believe they took him to Doullens, about nine miles away. They had him in handcuffs. Poor chap, I expect we won't see him again-almost certain to get shot.

**February 8th** Orders for all prisoners to do two hours pack drill, every day, then tied up to a tree for an hour.
They have cut our leave down, eighteen to go instead of thirty.
Weather very cold.

**February 9th** Heavy fall of snow last night.
We can get plenty of French beer. The local brew works out at four pence a bottle and Whitbread at ten pence.
We are very short of cigarettes and tobacco, as you cannot buy them in the village.

**February 10th** Very cold and the snow has turned to rain.
We managed to get some tobacco and papers, so the boys are making their own. They made one for "Daddy" Watkins and put

a small bit of cordite, with the tobacco. When he began to smoke it, it went off like a firework display.

**February 11th** We had a lovely dinner today as the Army Service Corps gave us a bag full of vegetables and a fowl . There are seventeen of us in the mess. So you can guess how much fowl we each had. It was a real treat, after so much bully beef and biscuits.

**February 12th and 13th** We are getting plenty of drill parades, three a day.
I have had no money this last two weeks, they tell me I am sixteen and eight pence in debt. Cannot explain how but I will write to the pay office.
We are getting plenty of rain, this last few days.
Very poor rations. If it wasn't for the A.S.C. we wouldn't have any vegetables at all.

**February 14th** Showery route march, in full marching order. Some of the boys have been ordered to clean their buttons. It's not right. We are out here for fighting, not show. Army red tape. No wonder the chaps grumble.

**February 15th to 19th** Still on our rest from the trenches. We have had five days of our usual rest : Route marches, drills, parades and training.

**February 20th and 21st** Enemy planes are busy about here today. Some bombs dropped, but very little damage and no casualties.
Hard frost.

**February 22nd** Very heavy fall of snow. We are having a bit of sport snow-balling.
One of the children of the French woman, at our farm billet, had something stuck in her throat. They couldn't dislodge it and the poor kid died. The mother is in a real state.

**February 23rd** Hard frost all night, but it started snowing again this morning, kept on until about 4pm. We had great fun rolling each other in it.
We have been ordered to clean our buttons while we stay here-more red tape. I don't know how we are going to clean them. Not one of us have any cleaning kit or any money to buy some.

**February 24th to 27th** This last week has been one of the severest we have had with snow every day, but it has now turned to rain.
Usual routine and the rations not very good.

**February 28th** Have orders to be ready to move at five minutes' notice. We have no idea where we are going.
The Seaforth Highlanders, who have been with us throughout the campaign, are moving to another Brigade. They came to wish us the best of luck. We get on well with them and we respect each other.

**1916 March**
**March 1st** Usual routine, weather fair but cold.

**March 2nd** More snowstorms.
The 12th Brigade who are part of our Division have come out of the trenches today, so it looks as if we are going to another part of the line.

**March 3rd and 4th** Usual routine.

**March 5th** All our artillery have come away from our old positions and now the whole Division is at rest. All leave is cancelled, so it looks as if we are in for some very serious work. Corporal Tynsdale went a bit balmy – he started shouting through the holes in the barn yesterday. They have taken him to hospital.

**March 6th to 16th** We have had ten days of the usual routine, with poor rations.
Quite a number of the chaps spend their spare time just wandering about. They don't seem to know what they are doing half the time. I think that the strain of waiting is proving too much for them.

**March 17th** Moved to Humbercamps, close to the firing line.
Our Division is to relieve the 37th Division.
Our 11th Battalion is part of the 37th Division. They are going for a rest.
This is one of the dirtiest places we have been in.
Lovely weather this last few days.

**March 18th** Heavy bombardment all night and plenty of rifle fire. A lot of aircraft on both sides reconnoitring all day long.
We move in reserve tomorrow starting at 9am.

***<u>Movement Orders by Lieut. Col. J. A.M. Bannerman, commanding 1st Battalion-Royal Warwickshire Regiment. Sat 18th March 1916.</u>***

*1. The Battalion will move to Bienvillers tomorrow the 19th .*
*2.Time of starting and route : Humbercamps - Pommier . Bienvillers*
*A coy 9.30 am B coy 9.45 am*
*C coy 10.00 am D coy 10.15 am*
*3 Men will march in steel helmets and carry their waterproof capes and leather jerkins.*
*4 Hostile Artillery. Each company will open out and march as platoons not less than 300 yards distance at the western entrance to Pommier.*
*5. Each company will be allocated one G.S. wagon for men's blankets and officer's heavy kit. These will be collected in the order in which the Coy's march off.*
*6. Each company will detail a loading party of 1 N.C.O. and 4 men to load these wagons and this party will go with their wagons to Bienvillers and see that it is unloaded at their respective billets.*
*7. Blankets - All blankets and officer's kit should be ready by 8.30 am The former to be rolled and stacked outside coy billets in bundles.*
*8. Billeting. Each company will detail the C.Q.M.S. and one man should parade at orderly room at 7.00 am under Lieut. F.N.H. Beamish.*
*9. Transport – Transport will follow in rear of last company and will march in single vehicles at 300 yard intervals on reaching Pommier. D.H. Willis. Lieut and adjutant, 1st battalion. R.W.R.*

**Transport wagons.**

**March 19th** A lovely morning.
The enemy shelled the road heavily where we were marching and Lance Corporal Cox was wounded.
One of our transport carts was blown up, killing both the horses. The Division had some remarkable escapes.
At about 11am we watched an aerial fight, but neither machine was brought down. As many as eight planes were fighting it out but we didn't see the result.
There has been plenty of shelling all day.

**March 20th** To the reserve billet at Bienvillers, which is just behind the firing line.
We were told that the A.S.C. driver who was wounded yesterday, has died from his wounds.
A large piece of shell from one of our own anti-aircraft guns crashed through the roof of our billet, but luckily no-one was hurt.
We are shelled quite heavily here.
A new draft of twenty four joined us today.

**March 21st** Heavy bombardment today. Our regiment had one killed and eleven injured.
We went into the firing line, at Monchy. We were under a shell bombardment on the road, but got in without casualties.
One of the Dublins told us that one of their sergeants had a bottle of rum in his dugout, so one of the chaps worked a plot to get it. He passed the word along, that the sergeant was wanted along the trench. While he was away, the chap pinched the rum. As he was bringing it away he met a fellow just coming up the trenches drunk, so he collared him and put him in the sergeant's dugout. When the sergeant came back, in a rage at being made a fool of, he saw this fellow in a drunken sleep. When he looked around and found his rum gone, he came to the conclusion that this fellow had drunk it. He put him under arrest.

**March 22nd** Raining.
About 7pm they opened heavy artillery fire, but luck was with us, no one was hit.
On fatigues, bringing up sandbags. It's pitch black dark, you can't see a hand in front of you. We kept falling in holes and got covered in mud. Poor old Spud was swearing like a trooper and lost half his load. He is supposed to be religious.
Another chap lost his hat when someone, carrying some boards, knocked it off. He couldn't strike a match out on top, to search for it. It took him ages to find it.
Had a tot of rum when we got back.

**March 23rd** Fairly quiet all day.
Mac and I, are on guard duty in the grenade magazine.
It started to snow at 1am and its perishing cold.
No rum issue tonight.

**March 24th** Heavy fall of snow.
Things are fairly quiet today.
They have a machine gun trained on the Battalion stores dump. We fetch the stores up at night and so far we have managed it without anyone getting hit.

**March 25th** Very cold and raining all day.
We were working at the dump when it got dark. Their machine gun opened up, firing blind. One of our chaps killed and two wounded.

**March 26th** Still cold and showery.
We get relieved tonight by the Dublins.
We went out at about 7pm.

**March 27th** Marched back to the billet in the village, without any casualties.
Sergeant Goodhall has been absent without leave for nearly ten weeks. Today, he re-joined us, so is on General Field Court Marshall. It looks like he will be getting shot.

**March 28th and 29th** Still very cold with snow showers.
Poor rations and we can't get vegetables for love nor money. It must be three weeks since we had any.
They shell this village nearly every day.
Tobacco is very scarce but we a getting a coffee bar shortly.

**March 30th** Fine morning. but cold.
Plenty of aeroplanes about. We have been watching a fight between two of them. The German won and unfortunately our chap came down behind the German lines.

Our Battalion played the 14th Heavy Battery at football. They only played a few minutes, when a shell dropped near the goal posts – luckily it did not explode. Our luck must have been in. Fine but cold.

**March 31st** A lovely spring day, fine and much warmer.
Two of the enemy planes bombed Humbercamps, which is a village about three miles behind us.
We are quite close to the front position here – our billet is about eight hundred yards from the German trenches.
We return to the firing line, at Monchy, tonight.
It only takes twenty minutes to get to our trench.
They shell the village every day.

**1916 April**
**April 1st** Very active all night.
They shelled our front line but did not do any damage.
Lots of aeroplanes flying about this morning.
Young Carter was wounded with shrapnel.
Heavy shelling again this afternoon, but we withdrew to the reserve trench until it eased off. Two chaps slightly wounded.

**April 2nd** Enemy artillery again very active.
They blew a section of our barbed-wire down but we went out and repaired it before daybreak.
We watched an aerial duel at about 11am. Our officer told us that the British aeroplane was a Vickers fighting plane. The German aeroplane, was shot down and fell behind his own lines.
Every night, as soon as it gets dark, the Battalion stores are sent up. A couple of us have to get them into the trenches,

ready to issue out to the Companies. It is very dangerous work as the dump is always under fire.
Last night, as we were unloading the trucks, they opened up with machine gun fire. We all dropped flat. "Lady" Hill dived and fell into a trench. Luckily he only got a few bruises. If we could have got into a rabbit hole we would have been thankful. The miracle was that no one got hit.

**April 3rd** Plenty of artillery duels. They don't give us much rest, at night.
The ration party of the Dublins, have diluted our rum issue. They must have filled the jar with dirty water. Our boys look like getting their own back when they carry the Dublins rations.

**April 4th** Cold and raining.
For the first time at this position, the enemy has started using minenwerfers. They are very high explosives. They leave a big crater, bigger than a Jack Johnson. We were very pleased when they had finished.
All leave cancelled again.

**April 5th** The enemy raided the 8th Battalion, on our right, capturing one of the Lewis rifles.
A retaliation raid was carried out during the night with bill-hooks and bombs. They caught one officer and twelve men. Our chaps had to return to their own trench as German reinforcements were advancing. The prisoners refused to come out of their trench with them so they killed the lot.
The next morning the Germans have put a notice on the wire "The first Warwicks we get hold of, will be roasted alive." Very promising, isn't it.

**April 6th** Cold and dull today.
They have been bombarding us all day with shells.
Two of the dugouts in our company were blown up, killing two and wounding two more.
It has been nearly three weeks since we had a change of underclothing. We are all feeling very scruffy and smelly.
We had some fun with "Mac". He went to sleep in the dugout and someone set fire to some rags close to him. They woke him up when the place was full of smoke and he thought he was getting gassed.
The weather is very cold again.
We get relieved out of the firing line tonight.

**April 7th** Terrific bombardment on the right.
We have been told they attempted an attack but got repulsed.
The weather has been a treat today.
Had a bath and change of underclothes.

**April 8th** Mac, who is a bit hard of hearing, came running in the billet, telling us that paper man was coming down the road. They always blow a horn for identification but all that Mac had heard was a donkey braying.
Lance Corporal Bird was due for leave at 3.30am this morning, but he didn't wake up and missed the draft. We have really pulled his leg about it today.
One of our airmen who we call the "mad Major" has been flying very low over the German lines. They opened rifle and machine gun fire but the cheeky bounder opened fire with his machine guns. It's a miracle they did not fetch him down.

**April 9th** The enemy has hardly fired a shot all day.

There has been a few of our aeroplanes about, they don't fire unless they can help it, in case they are spotted by observers.

**April 10th** Rained like the devil all day and very cold.
Sergeant Goodhall was reduced to the ranks, and is to serve ten years imprisonment, when the war is over. The charge, at the Court Marshall read : "Desertion for a period of ten weeks"

**April 11th** Raining all day.
The Germans very quiet.
The "Jocks" on our left captured a sap, about midnight.

**April 12th** Relieved the Dublins at 5.30pm. We got wet through as it's been pouring down all day. The enemy has been quiet.

**April 13th** Very stormy weather.
Mad Jack, as we call him, a very daring aeroplane pilot was out at daybreak. It's a wonder how his aeroplane kept flying, as the wind was so strong. He soon had to go back.
Leave has been cancelled again and message sent out for all men to re-join their units by the 18th, so it looks as if we are in for a rough time again.

**April 14th** We have been kept busy making a new supply dump this last three days.
We are going to try to take one of the enemy saps. I believe it comes off tonight. Let's hope the boys have the best of luck.
It had to be cancelled as it was a moonlight night.

**April 15th** Very cold and hailstorms.
Our artillery bombarded the enemy at 3pm, they retaliated, but very little damage done, with no casualties.

An aeroplane was flying over the lines at 10pm, but we could not tell whose it was.
A very moonlight night.

**April 16th** A lovely morning, but cold.
Turned to rain about 10pm.
Both sides have been very quiet all day.

**April 17th** Very wet and stormy.
At about 3.15pm our artillery opened a very heavy bombardment on the German trenches.
At 4pm our bombers advanced to the German trench. They got in and threw their bombs into their dugouts. Heavy groans were heard. The Germans were very numerous, so we retired to our own trench. We were only allowed fifteen minutes to get there and back, and only sustained one casualty.
At the same time the R.I.R. carried out a similar raid. They counted three officers and thirteen men dead in the trench.
Both raids were very successful.
Later in the day Sergeant Hobbs and Corporal Hogg were blown up by an aerial torpedo. Both of them were very good fellows.

**April 18th.** Rain all day and night.
The General and Staff congratulated us on our raid yesterday.
To be relieved out of the trenches tonight.
Poor rations.

**April 19th and 20th.** Terrible weather, raining day and night.
We played the Lewis rifles at football but we had to chuck it in, as it was raining too hard. We were leading 1-0.
Bacon only issued twice a week.

**April 21st** (Good Friday) Still raining.
Every time we are out of the trenches I organise a crib handicap. I won it myself this time.

**April 22nd** More rain, we shall soon get swamped.
The Huns have been very active since the raid, but they get more than they give.
Lieutenant Shoot and Private Hazel, were trying out a new type of bomb but it exploded too soon, wounding both of them slightly.

**April 23rd** Lovely morning and plenty of aeroplanes about.
One of our shells burst just leaving the muzzle, (what they call a primitive burst) and a chap from the Cyclist Corps was killed.

**April 24th** Lovely day, bright and sunny.
Orders came in that some of our planes will be marked with a black stripe on their wings instead of the usual rings.
Marched up to the trenches at Monchy at 5pm. We had only been back five minutes, when a shell blew the B. Company servants dugout to bits. One of the chaps killed and five injured.
At 9pm we had to go back to the village for rations.

**April 25th** A splendid day.
The enemy have got a lot more artillery in front of us, and they have been giving us a really rough time We have had about twenty casualties this last two days and four dugouts blown up. The constant shelling is playing havoc with some of the chap's nerves. They have managed to put two guns of our heavy battery out of action.
An Engineers' officer arrested one of the civilians. The man had staked 3 cows in the field opposite the battery, with their heads

facing the guns. We know that there are many spies about and this looked highly suspicious.
Twelve months ago today we were at the big battle, at Ypres, where we lost over seven hundred of the best.

**April 26th** They have been giving us a heavy artillery bombardment again, but very little damage done and no casualties.
Scotty and I spotted a hare, watched it for a long time waiting to get a shot at it, but it didn't come near enough. We had visions of a really good supper.

**April 27th** During the night a horse strayed near the lines and the Huns had a real go at it. They started with machine gun fire but didn't hit it and then sent a high explosive shell. It burst near the horse and it galloped off like mad. We haven't seen it since.
The H.Q. staff servants lit a fire to do some cooking and the enemy spotted the smoke. They came under heavy shellfire but no one was hit.
I had a piece of shrapnel drop at my feet, another lucky miss.
Lieutenant Brecknell lost two fingers with shrapnel.
The Sergeant cook sent some rice duff up the line. We could have hit him with it, it was just like a stone slab.

**April 28th** Very busy with shelling.
Two of our aeroplanes went over the enemy lines and forced two of their observation balloons to descend. They have put up two searchlights, in their place, for night work.

**April 29th** Heavy artillery duels.
Some of our aircraft are out during the night, spotting for enemy artillery. They signal to our batteries by firing their guns.
Weather still very good.

**April 30th** Still keeping up heavy artillery duels. We had three of B. Company blown to bits.
The Hun have just shouted over that General Townsend and one thousand, five hundred men have been captured by the Turks.
We don't know whether to believe them or not.
The General in Command of the 37th Division has been arrested, as a spy. When we relieved the 37th, at this position, we thought it peculiar that our division have had more casualties in five weeks than the 37th Divisions had in nine months.

**1916 May**
**May 1st** Special orders to vacate this position today.
We were relieved, at 9pm, by the King's Royal Rifles.
We marched to a place named St. Amand and stayed there for the night. The boys are glad of a change, as it has been very rough fighting here.
We had about forty casualties in the last six days.

**May 2nd** Marched about ten miles, to Halloy and stayed the night.
We have no idea where we are going to.
Very hot day.

**May 3rd** Marched through Doullens to Neuvillette.
I begin to think we have become a flying column. We shall be glad when we are finished with all this marching about.

**May 4th** Another lovely day.
Had a full inspection of kit.
At 11pm orders came through to be ready to move off at 8.30am tomorrow.
My feet are sore but I hope to manage the march, with a bit of luck.

**May 5th** Marched about twenty kilometres to Agenville.
It was a very hot day and about a hundred and forty fell out - so you can guess how rough it was. I managed to stick at it, but my feet are very sore.

**May 6th** This is the first time any British troops have been here, so the folks have made a real fuss of us.
They sold out of all the beer in the village the first day, but plenty of cider here.

**May 7th** Change of weather, very much colder today.
We have managed to buy a few eggs here, two pence each.

**May 8th** Raining nearly all day.
McGee got five years imprisonment for being absent from the firing line.
Orders to clean our buttons.

**May 9th to 13th** Doing Battalion training and also smoke helmet drills.

This is a poor village and you cannot buy anything to eat, and can only buy wine to drink.
It has been raining hard this last four days.

**May 14th** Orders to hand all our blankets into stores.
Kit inspection and drill.

**May 15th** Can hardly sleep as it's so cold without blankets.
Raining again today.

**May 16th** Splendid day.
We are still out of the trenches doing battalion training.
I expect they are keeping us in reserve for something hot.
Wine is one franc, six cents a bottle.

**May 17th** Another fine day.
Battalion training.

**May 18th** The Brigade held it's sports day.
Our Battalion won the quarter mile and the horse jumping.
Two of the transport chaps won some minor events.
It was a lovely day.

**May 19th** No entry made.

**May 20th** Usual routine of training.

**May 21st** We marched twelve kilometres, to Gapennes.
We had to do a mock attack on the way, under aerial observation. It was a very warm day.

**May 22nd to 24th** Plenty of Canadian Cavalry around here. We are doing some special training. I expect it is for some big offensive move this summer.
We are billeted in a barn near to a big château. It is in such a very dirty condition that we prefer to sleep out in the open.

**May 25th** We had a boxing and singing concert tonight. It was quite a change and we all enjoyed it.
It was slightly spoiled because we couldn't get a drink of beer. The weather is lovely.

**May 26th** The parson has gone, on his horse, to try and see if he get some beer for the boys. He is a good old stick.
Very heavy training today so they must be getting us fit for some rough work.

**1916 June**

**May 27th to June 3rd** Regular routine of drill and training. Orders to be ready to move tomorrow.

**June 4th** Marched about twenty two kilometres to Fienvillers. It was a stiff day. We are were all about done in.
We are only stopping here for the night.

**June 5th** We marched to a wood, three kilometres beyond Authie, twenty six kilometres altogether.
We are all dead beat, but I feel very proud that only seven men fell out, especially as it was raining hard some of the way.
If anyone had pushed the front section of four, it would have knocked the whole of the Battalion over. We were all so foot sore.

**June 6th to 8th** Getting plenty of rain.
We are sleeping in a big wood.
"Porky" killed a young rook, feathered and cooked it.
Young Guest is trying to clean a bike with a toothbrush, but he's not making much progress.
Leave has been cut down again. Only six going home, this week, getting five days instead of seven.

**June 9th** Still raining hard.
There are men and guns coming up here, as fast as they can.
I believe we are going to try to make a big advance very shortly.

**June 10th** Battalion training.
It is still raining.

**June 11th** Still raining.
We have been to a place, where we have been able to get a bath (first one for nearly two months).
We are to move to a place called Bertrancourt tonight.

**June 12th** Arrived at Bertrancourt at 10.30pm.
We are wet through because it is still raining.
We are sleeping in huts, and the whole place is a sea of mud.

**June 13th** Orders to move this morning and we moved to Mailly- Maillet, arriving at dinner time.
It's been pouring with rain all night and day.
We pitched some tents to sleep in but the ground is soaking wet. Five of our fellows have gone on patrol duty, so it leaves me in charge of the regimental police.
I think they are away for a week or so.

**June 14th** Still raining.
We are hard at work making room for men in the firing line, for a big advance in the near future.
They put all the clocks on one hour, tonight at 11pm.
This will rob us of an hour's shut eye.

**June 15th** Only sending two men on leave instead of twelve.
Had three wounded this last three nights on working parties.
Very rough weather and keeping very cold.
Ginger Kimberley got seven days No.2 field punishment for being absent without leave.

**June 16th** Cold rain.
We are digging in the trenches, until about 3.30am, making preparations for an offensive. Everything will be ready in a week or so.

**June 17th** Fine day but rough.
Met a fellow called Pitcock, in the Rifle Brigade. He works on the trams and we had quite a chat about the old times.
Plenty of aeroplanes about today.

**June 18th** Marched to the trenches at 2.45pm.
We went the wrong way. Eventually, we got there after going miles out of our way.
We watched two aeroplane duels.
We are at Auchonvillers.

**June 19th** Our trenches have been named the "White City", because the soil is like cement. We look more like bakers than soldiers.
The dugout is called "River Clyde", on account of there always being plenty of water in it.

**June 20th** Splendid day.
Plenty of aerial duels. One of our planes was shot down over the German lines.
We are all ready for a big advance.
We have had some casualties today, ten killed or wounded.
Read about the great Russian advance.

**June 21st** Another splendid day.
They have been shelling us all day. One killed and another wounded, this morning.
There is a rumour about a peace conference, but we don't really believe it.

**June 22nd** Another real summer's day.
Things have been rather quiet today.
We have got everything ready for a big offensive.
I expect it will come off in a few days.

**June 23rd** The weather has broken, raining hard all day.
The rations are poor. As many as seven or eight in some companies have to share a loaf. Perhaps they cannot bring the rations up.

**June 24th** Stormy weather.
The artillery have been bombarding all day so this must be the start of the offensive. Let's hope that we have plenty of luck.
Under heavy artillery fire that started at about 11.30pm.
The Royal Engineers gave the enemy a dose of gas, but the wind changed direction, causing some of our own chaps to get gassed.

It has been a Devil's night, nearly half the front-line blown in by high explosive shells and we have sixty wounded and dead.
A night of horror.

**June 25th** The enemy bombardment continues.
We have been standing ready all night and day, in case they attack.
Our Engineers came up again to mount a gas attack, but one of the tanks got hit by shrapnel and started to leak. We had a lot of our chaps gassed and fourteen of them have died from the effects. It's been sheer hell here for the last three days.
To date we estimate about a hundred casualties.
My dear old chum Butch was blown to pieces this morning. May I live to see him avenged. He was a dear old chap.

**June 26th** Still bombarding.
Most of the chaps are fairly done in with the gas and bombardment but they have stuck it well.
We are being relieved tonight for a short rest.
Raining again.

**June 27th** Still raining.
Marched back for a rest to Battalion base camp.
The doctor has sent a whole batch of the chaps to hospital.
There are a lot more who are not well, but won't go because they want to see the finish of the big offensive.

**June 28th** The General gave us an inspection.
He thanked us for our work over the last few days and told us that he was relying on us for the offensive starting tomorrow.
Later we are told that the offensive is to be held back for a day or two.

About two hundred more men arrived today. It looks as if the enemy are going to get a real battle this time.

**June 29th** A great deal of aerial activity. Many aircraft about and we just counted the observation balloons, eighteen of ours and two of the Huns.
Our artillery are bombarding heavily and a batch of about forty from the enemy, gave themselves up.
This morning very showery weather.

**June 30th** Orders to march to the assembly trenches tonight, ready for the offensive tomorrow.
We had a church service this evening, but all I can say is that the chaps are all out to do their best, for the sake of the folks at home. Let's hope that we all have the best of luck.

**Map 3 : Frontline map July to Oct 1916**

***THE BATTLE OF THE SOMME.***

***July 1st 1916 : Official narrative of Operations.***

*At 9.10 am on July 1st the Battalion advanced in small column formation from assembly trenches across the open in support of the 2nd R. Dublin Fusiliers 1/R Irish being on their left. At 9.15 received an order that the battalion was to halt and reform at Tenderloin. Arrived and reformed there by 10.00 am. The left Coy (C) had advanced to a position just in rear of the front line before the order to halt has reached them. At 10.05 am received an order to make an attempt to reach the German line at point 27 as British troops were reported in and around point 59. I sent a strong patrol under Lieut. R.R. Walkers from A coy to try and make a lodgement at point 27, moving across by Watling street. This patrol got across to about Q4b 8 ½ 2 where they were stopped by intense machine gun fire from Beaumont Hamel and had to return, arriving back in our line at 2.15 pm.*

*My intention was that if this patrol could have made a lodgement at point 27, to send over the remainder of A Coy in small parties with a supply of bombs and bomb along the German line. At about 1.45 pm an order was received to stop any attempt to gain a lodgement at point 27. I cancelled the order but too late to stop the patrol.*

*At 2.30 pm sent 1 Coy up to the front line to hold our original line at about Q4b – 4.5 to fill up a gap in the line at this point.*

*At 7.15 pm had orders to relieve the troops along our front line from maxim trench to Q4/12 2 Coy's in front line, the remainder in support, the relief being completed by 11.30 pm Casualties from this period 8 officers, 250 other ranks.*

*5.7.16 G.M.B. Forster, Lt Col*
*1st btn. R Warwickshire Regt.*
*A Coy, Auchonvillers.*

**1916 July**

**July 1st.** A great offensive.

At 6am, all our artillery opened a rapid bombardment. They kept it up until 7.30. The engineers fired a mine under Beaumont Hamel but it did not appear to be a success.

At 7.30 the 11th Brigade started to advance.

At about 9 they had taken the Germans third line and we then went through them and continued the advance. Altogether we advanced two and half miles.

All at once the enemy received reinforcements but we still held our ground.

About 11.30 the 29th Division were forced back and the Germans advanced. That put our flank in great danger but we still held on. We suddenly got terrible inflated fire of machine guns and shrapnel, on our flanks. Our chaps were falling like skittles.

We then dropped back into their 3rd line trench. They then threw another attack against us but we stuck like glue.

In the meantime, the enemy had encircled our flank with the intention of cutting us off. It was terrible, just wholesale murder. The only chance we had of getting out of it was to hang on until dark, and try to get the chaps back. The chaps told the General that they weren't going to give up, what they fought so hard to get.

We managed to get back under the cover of darkness. It seemed terrible, to have to leave the wounded men, behind but we have to obey orders. I think that if we had tried to get them away, we would have been wiped out. As it was, we lost more than half the Division. What terrible luck, after getting them on the run, to be robbed of victory through the fault of a Division on your flank. This Division was a crack at Gallipoli, but perhaps they did their very best.

We have been getting in the wounded as well as we can all night, but I'm afraid there is a lot more of the poor brave lads. God help them.
We are fairly done up. Had no sleep for the last two days. Hope they will send us a relief tonight.

**July 2nd** Everyone has said how well we did to stick it out and they didn't expect any of us to get back alive.
We have tried again to get in the dead and wounded, but the Huns do not give us a chance and some of the poor chaps have been out, this last forty eight hours.
They have sent what's left of the Division in reserve, with the exception of the Irish Fusiliers and ourselves.
I feel really done in, we have had no sleep this last three days and nights.
Only biscuits and bully beef.

**July 3rd** The General has told us we have done more than was expected. He said our Division was very unfortunate that the enemy has concentrated its troops in our sector – our division was up against three of the enemy's. We are now expecting a counter-attack, so we are standing to and not getting chance of a nap.

***Official Press Bureau Report : July 3rd 1916.***
*The Anglo French offensive on the Western front continues to produce highly encouraging results. It is reported from British Quarters that following our capture of Montauban and Manetz our troops had carried Fricourt and that despite the stubborn resistance of the enemy, satisfactorily progress has been made in other directions.*
*Heavy losses have been inflicted on the enemy and so far 9,500 prisoners have been taken, 6,000 by the French and 3,500 by*

*the British. The troops are in excellent spirits and it is reported that as a result of very effective artillery fire, our casualties are not heavy.*

**July 4th** They have been shelling us very heavily, but so far no counter-attack.
We are told that it was through our efforts, pinning the enemy down, that our troops on the extreme left were able to continue their advance.
We do not know how the battle is progressing in other parts of the British line, but it is rumoured that the British are having some success.
Terrible weather. Up to your neck in mud.

**July 5th** Heavy artillery bombardment all night and day and at about 3.00 am all the shelling stopped for a short time.
Managed to get a good night's sleep last night.
Some of the medical corps went out and brought in the dead and wounded. Six of the wounded has been out for three nights and four days. Poor chaps, they are in a terrible state but we think that five of them will live.

**July 6th** We are still having a rough time, being under constant heavy shelling. The noise is making us all tired out.
To make things worse food rations are very scarce. We shall soon all be shadows.
At about 11.30pm they dropped a big shell, no more than ten yards from where we stood. Two of the chaps were killed and nineteen wounded. My luck is still with me.
Orders to be relieved tonight.

**July 7th** Splendid weather, both sides bombarding heavily. We have been flooded out coming out of the trenches today.
The communication trenches are up to our waists in water. We got soaked coming back out of the line.
They shelled the place we stopped in at night, so we had to clear out before morning. We are now in a wood by Mailly-Maillet.

**July 8th** The Corps Commander inspected us this morning. He made us feel rather proud. He told us that General Joffre had specially congratulated our Division, for our splendid part in the big battle. He said we fought that well that the Germans had to send all their reserves to stop us, which had allowed the French troops on our right to gain their ground with scarcely any resistance.
We suffered very heavily, our division had some seven thousand wounded or killed.

**July 9th** Nice weather.
Last night was the first good night's sleep for eight days.
It seemed a godsend to have a good wash.
We were due to be issued with new clothes today but they haven't come through.
I have only had this shirt on for a month! so I could do with a change.
The rations have been good.

**July 10th to 12th** Fairly good weather.
We are getting fairly good grub after our rough time. We can't get any vegetables for love nor money.
Had a draft of fifty from home.

**July 13th** On fatigues last night, taking gas cylinders up to the front line. Looks like dirty work again shortly.
We boiled a piece of meat last night intending to have it for our breakfast. In the night it was stolen. 'Oh, for his blood'.

**July 14th** No entry made.

**July 15th** Relieved the Dublins in the firing line.
We are still getting plenty of heavy shelling.
Last night our transport section got hit, killing one man and four horses, and two were wounded.
Getting poor rations.

**July 16th** Still the bombardment goes on.
Poor rations and wet.

**July 17th** Relieved by the King's Own.
It's been raining hard this last twenty four hours. We got wet through. Up to our knees in mud and water coming through the communication trenches.
We dare not go back over the top as there is a heavy bombardment.

**July 18th** A stormy day.
Two chaps on General Field Court Martial for cowardice. One of them refused to go over the parapet in the advance on July 1st, then ran away. He was caught on the 15th, hiding in the sunken road.

**July 19th** Rations much better, had a good wash and clean-up and a long rest at the camp on Bertrancourt – Acheux Road.

**July 20th** Sudden orders to move.
We marched to Beauval, arriving at about 8pm. All footsore and hungry.
It seems to be a very big town.

***<u>The Battle of the Somme : July to November.1916</u>***

*From Sir Douglas Haig in his despatch of Dec 23 1916.after the joint offensive of the Somme.*
*The object of the offensive was threefold:*
*1. To relieve the pressure on the French at Verdun.*
*2. To assist our allies in other theatres of war by stopping any further transfer of German troops from the Western Front.*
*3. To wear down the strength of the force opposed to us. To quote his own words: "This has been one of the greatest if not absolutely the greatest struggle that has ever taken place." Our troops faced a formidable task. Along the whole of the German front situated on high undulating ground with the advantage of the position almost everywhere in their favour, the enemy had strong fortification. Several lines of deep trenches protected by barbed wire entanglements, many in two belts up to 40 yards broad. The woods, villages and mills were fortified and in the villages many deep cellars were supplemented by deep dugouts and communication tunnels, with defensive mine fields. "These defences formed in short, not merely a series of successive lines, but one composite system of enormous depth and strength. Behind this second system of trenches, woods, villages and other strong points prepared for defence, the enemy had several other lines already completed and aerial reconnaissance confirmed further trenches being dug even further back,"*
*On July 1st nearly 100,000 troops marched forward. The wire had not been broken but merely gapped by the bombardment and this left the British troops massing by the gaps, a perfect*

*target for the German machine gunners, who were heavily entrenched. The British losses for this one day were over 57,000, including 20,000 killed in action. This figure represent approximately 60% of the officers and 40% of the men involved in the action. When Sir Douglas Haig heard of the figure some three days later he decided to concentrate on the right and proceed on a smaller front.*

***A short summary of operations for the period July to October.***

***On July 11th 1917 Sir Douglas Haig wrote:*** *"After 10 days and nights of continuous fighting our troops have completed the methodical capture of the whole of the enemy's 1st system of defence on a front of 1,400 yards. This system consisted of numerous and continuous lines of fire trenches, supporting trenches and reserve trenches, extending to various depths from 2,000 to 4,000 yards and including 5 strongly fortified villages, numerous heavily wired and entrenched woods and a number of extremely strong redoubts.*

*The capture of each of these trenches represents an operation of some importance and the whole of them are now in our hands." The latter end of July and the month of August were dominated by localised offensives in small fronts for strategic purposes. No general push had been attempted but much ground had been gained. Sir Douglas Haig : "In this way our line was brought up to the front crest of the ridge above Martinpuich and Pozieres Windmill and the high ground north of the village was secured and with them, observation over the enemy's gun positions in their neighbourhood and around le Sars."*

*The method of attack in small sections continued in early September with major successes.*

**July 21st** In billets.
Have orders to move out at 11pm tonight.
Didn't get a chance to see the town.

**July 22nd** Moved to Candas, at 11pm but got lost on the road in the pitch black dark. We went about five miles out of our way. Entrained at about 2.30am, but have no idea where we are going.

**July 23rd** Got out of the train at Poperinge, this is near Ypres. Another very hot spot – they call it the cock pit. We are in the same Army Corps as the famous Guards.
They thought that we had just come out. They curled up when someone told them that we just come from the "Battle of the Somme".

**July 24th** We are billeted in a big standing camp just on the Watao Road outside Poperinge.
We have orders to scrub our straps...more red tape.
The Prince of Wales came through our camp today, but very few people seemed to recognise him.

**July 25th** Feeling rough today.
I have a touch of fever. I will have to starve it out.
I nearly got tipsy on some English beer, so I will sweat the fever out instead.
Oh for a change in clothing, I have had this on now for nearly six weeks,

**July 26th** Relieved the Grenadier Guards on the notorious Canal bank.
It has not altered much in the way it looks but it is not such a death trap as it used to be.

**July 27th** Relieved the Irish Guards, in the front line by La Brique.
We hadn't been here five minutes before Waring of A. Company was killed. This place is a death trap.
Had to bring up the rations from the village.

**July 28th** Just after midnight the enemy tried to surprise us with a bombing party, but we caught them in the act.
We killed three of them and the remainder scuttled away. They were armed with bombs and a new type of rifle with a magazine that holds twenty rounds.
We have got a plague of mosquitoes. When they bite you all your flesh swells up. They cause malaria fever.

**July 29th** Enemy fairly quiet.
Two Germans came out on patrol but they never got back.
We had to cut the grass in front of us as it's that long the Germans creep up to you, before you can spot them. They will soon find the difference. Apparently, they regularly used to creep up on the Guards.

**July 30th** We have been having lovely summer weather this last few days, but the mosquitoes are a menace.
It is very unhealthy here, on account of so many bodies being buried just under the surface. You can't dig anywhere without coming across some poor devil.

**July 31st** We are getting casualties on ration and digging parties. They keep the machine guns firing all night. The enemy hit one of our machine guns but only slightly wounded two men.

**1916 August**

**August 1st** Lovely summer's day.
It's been fairly quiet all day.
This afternoon I was washing my shirt, in a big tub of water and sitting on another tub with a plank across. The plank slipped and I fell in the water, backside first. The chaps thought it was a great joke and wanted to know if it was a new way of diving.

**August 2nd and 3rd** Splendid weather.
We have been on the alert expecting a gas attack this last two nights but so far it has not come.
The General congratulated us on our good work in this position. He told us that the enemy in front were, the notorious Jaquers, the lot that ransacked Louvain.

**August 4th** Relieved from the trenches.
We are in a camp at Vlamertinghe, about seven miles back. It is a terrible place for water, it all has to be brought up – Strict rationing and can't even have a wash.

**August 5th** Lovely weather.
At about 10am Lieutenant Gordon was giving a lecture about bombs. He had one in his hand which was supposed to be a dummy. He was showing them how it worked when it suddenly exploded, wounding fourteen men – two of them died later.

**August 6th to 9th** Routine training and rest period.
General Plumer inspected us. He was congratulating us about our great work on the Somme.
We couldn't help but notice that not one of us got even a military medal. They don't seem to think the old regular Regiments want them.

At 11pm the enemy carried out a gas attack. The 11st Brigade lost about two hundred and fifty men.
They also attacked us but were easily repulsed.

**August 10th** Orders back to the firing line.

**August 11th** We relieved the East Lancs in the firing line, near Boesinghe.
They shell this place regularly and also gas every time the wind is in their favour.
Our Colonel fell in a mud pond this morning, didn't dare laugh until he had gone.

**August 12th** They have been shelling the Canal bridges but no damage done.
We still have a big problem with water.
Whatever drop we get, they bring up at night, in petrol cans.
We will soon be eaten alive by the mosquitos.
Some of the boys caught some eels in the canal, but after looking at the state of the water I just would not eat them.
Orders to be relieved tonight.

**August 13th and 14th** Marched back for a rest, at Trois Tours, from the firing line.
Still very short of water.

**August 15th** Went in reserve to Château Brielen.
They shell it regularly.
The officers told us that in peace time it belonged to von Bissell, the man who sentenced Nurse Edith Cavell.

**August 16th** Stormy weather.
Still at the château.
The enemy has been very active all day.
At about midnight we had a gas alarm but it proved a failure because the wind was too strong for the dirty bounders.

**August 17th** Orders to move the Battalion.

**August 18th 19th 20th**. We are in support at a château .
There is a bit of fishing here.
So I have been trying my luck. The first day caught a sandbag and plenty of weeds, second day nothing and the third caught 2 small eels.
Just my luck we are moving tonight and it has been raining like the devil this last few days.
We parade at 9.30pm.
The Battalion entrained but the headquarters staff walked.

**August 21st** Arrived at our destination at Poperinge at 1.30am this morning.
The last part of the journey across country – it was very muddy and slippery, but I was one of the people who did not fall down this time.

**August 22nd** We relieved the Canadians in trenches near Hill 60.
This is the worst place on the whole western front, only a few yards separate us from the enemy and we are bombing each other night and day.
We have to stand to our posts all night.

**August 23rd to 25th** No record made.

**August 26th** This is hell.
No rest at all and the smell is enough to knock you down.
The Canadians must have been too scared to go out and bury their muck.
It's filthy here and the bombing continues night and day.
A few sent away with fever.
Showery weather.

**August 27th** They have been bombarding us very heavily, with shells, grenades, bombs, trench mortars and everything you can mention.
We have only had six casualties.
It took our artillery half an hour before they retaliated and even when they did, they did not use the heavies.
You should hear the boys crib.

**August 28th and 29th** Very heavy bombardment, both days, on each side.
We have been very lucky - four of us got moved out from our dugout into another dugout. The next day the dugout we had left got hit with a shell.
Rainstorms both days.

**August 30th and 31st** We exploded a mine crater at 2am but it was too shallow to occupy it.
Three or four chaps were buried when it exploded but they got nothing more than a slight shock.
We got relieved at 9pm, but came under heavy bombardment.
It was raining like the devil and we had to walk thirteen kilometres.
The enemy made a gas attack as we were leaving but it was a failure as the wind got too strong.

We arrived at the camp at 3am. (Vlamertinghe, Oudenaarde Rd.)

**1916 September**

**September 1st 2nd and 3rd** Weather picking up.
We are told that the Anzacs are coming to this position.
One of the boys was getting some water out of the stream when he fell in. I don't know how he will get his kit dry. There was no sun out.
They gassed this position at 11pm but they did not attack.

**September 4th** Marched to a camp near Poperinge on the Proven Rd.
I believe we are down here for a week or two's rest from the trenches.
It has been raining all day.

**September 5th and 6th** We are doing some very hard training. I expect we are in for some hot work when our rest is over.
There was an aeroplane flying about late last night but do not know who it belonged to.

**September 7th** A fine day but very windy.
A big squad, about thirty of our aeroplanes, passed here on a bombing raid over the German lines.
It must be very risky work and we wish them luck.

**Big Squadron of our aeroplanes.**

**September 8th** Our Regimental football team played the Royal Welsh and won 5-0.
The Quartermaster sergeant of B. Company on Field General Court Martial for stealing a watch off a chap who he found fast asleep.

**September 9th** Regular routine of military training.

**September 10th** The Corps Commander inspected us.
He told us the usual tale of how splendid the Regiment had been. Orders for two hundred of us to go out digging tonight somewhere on the railway line, where it has been blown up with shells.
Marched off at 6.30pm

**September 11th** Very rough weather.
We spent the night digging to repair the railway line and arrived back at 5.30am.
This is to be a regular thing, sending two hundred men of the regiment each night.
We had one wounded last night.

**September 12th to 13th** Routine military training.

**September 14th** Very cold and showery.
The Transport Section challenged the Headquarters staff to a football match.
We played this afternoon and beat them, 7-1. We didn't half rag them. I don't expect that they ever play us again.

**September 15th** Miserable wet weather again.
D. Company challenged us to a football match.
We beat them 2-1 and their goal was scored by one of our chaps.
The adjutant gave our team a five franc note each.

**September 16th** At 10.30am we had a sudden order to parade for General's inspection.
He told us that they wanted us down south again.
The same old tale - no regiment like ours, sorry to see us go, and all that.
The Colonel has been recommended for promotion to Brigadier General because of **our** good work.

**September 17th** Marched to Proven where we entrained at 1am. After going through Calais and Boulogne we arrived at Amiens at about 3pm .
We then marched twelve kilometres to Colsy.

The chaps are worn out, nothing to eat or drink since tea yesterday.

**September 18th to 23rd** Military training at a camp near Colsy. We all expect to be in a big attack very soon.
The weather has been vile over the last three days.

**September 24th** Marched fourteen kilometres to Corbie and were billeted in a French peasant's home overnight.
We managed to get a drink or two and got the children to sing French songs to us.
It all made a very nice change.
Back to the Somme district again.

**September 25th** Marched to Mericourt in lovely weather.
Plenty of Hun prisoners at work mending the roads.
German aeroplanes over in the night dropping bombs.
We had four killed and a few wounded.

***Official Narrative summary : September 25th*** *The start of the attack to secure the entire ridge to give depth against any enemy counter attack the following spring and to hide from the enemy's view the activities behind the line.*
*For similar reasons it was important to capture the enemy points above the Ancre from which the German Army could look down the river valley to Albert.*
*From September 24th British troops and French troops combined for the attack.*

**September 26th** We are here in support of the Cavalry but it is hard to say when we will get into action.
We had a swimming parade this afternoon, but the water was too cold to stay in long.

The weather has bucked up.

**September 27th to 29th** Military training and rest.

**September 30th** Marched to Daours and on route carried out training, signalling to and from our aeroplanes.
Next week we go into action again.
I believe we have to try to take a fortified village.

**1916 October**
**October 1st to 5th** No entries made.

***Official report : Summary of operations.***
*October 2nd Incessant rain had brought mud and slime to such proportions that a major attack was impractical, so costly localised attacks took place.*

**October 6th** The Sergeant and myself caught a deserter of the 19th Battalion Cheshires.
He had escaped from three guardrooms.
He swore he would escape from ours, so we put him in irons so he couldn't escape.
Orders to move tonight.

**October 7th** Marched to Meaulte, near Mametz.
This was in the German's hands in July.
It is pouring down with rain and we are having a rough time

**October 8th and 9th** At Mansel Camp near Mametz.
It is on the way to the front.
We got into position about 6.30pm, to relieve the London Rifle Brigade.

They have tried to take a position near Le Transloy, but have failed twice.
I believe we have to try and take it.
Shelling very heavy night and day. It is like hell itself, here.
Plenty of German dead lying about but we have no time to bury them.
I hope that we have the luck to take this very strong position.

**October 10th** Fine bright day.
Our aircraft have been busy, all day.
There have been a lot of duels in the air.
We counted thirty four of our planes, at one time.
One of our pilots got hit, but the observer brought it down behind our lines.
Unfortunately, on landing it tipped over on its back.
One of our airman bought a German plane down in flames at their own lines.
They must have been burnt alive.
Very short of water here.
The nearest village is Les Boeufs.

**October 11th** Rainstorms.
It is too rough for aircraft but the bombardment is terribly heavy. Today, we have had about seventy casualties.
We attack tomorrow, time to be notified later.

**(The battle of Transloy Ridge)**
**October 12th** Our artillery opened up a steady bombardment early this morning.
They kept increasing and it built up until you could feel the earth moving.
At 2.05pm we attacked a very strong position. A ridge that commands Le Transloy at Bapaume.

We got there all right and started to dig in but the R.I.F. on our left retired, causing us to get inflated fire.
This was too fierce so we were ordered to retire about four hundred yards.
We then dug in at this new position and made it good.
Altogether we won about five hundred yards.
This position has been attacked five times, but we are the only Brigade that has succeeded.
We had about two hundred and fifty casualties today but feel very proud to have reached this point.
Had the weather been better we should have had support from our aeroplanes to help us. We had also expected two tanks but none came.

**October 13th** The Huns artillery has been bombarding us all day but our own artillery have been covering us well.
We are holding the position easily, with only slight damage.
About 5.30pm they made a counter-attack on our left.
Our guns were too good for them so they were repulsed.
Relieved at 10pm and went into reserve.
Everyone is fairly done in for want of a rest.
We have not been able to get any water to have a wash for five days.

**October 14th to 16th** Standing by in reserve at Guillemont.
Our artillery are bombarding, day and night.
We have had plenty of shells here, but only slight damage.
The continual noise of the guns, is really getting on everyone's nerves.
In nearly every village, which we have taken, there isn't even a wall standing and what was once woods, only the tree trunks are left. So you can guess what the artillery fire was like.

**Mud and water with trees. (Chateau wood.)**

**October 17th to 21st** Very wet and cold at night.
It's so cold the chaps can't sleep unless they are dog tired.
There was such a sharp frost, one night, they had to issue us a blanket each, before everyone reported sick with frostbite.
Over the last five days we have been in reserve at Bernafay wood and been expecting to be called into action.

***Short Summary of Operations October 1st to 20th :***
*The battle of Transloy ridge.*
*Attacks were carried out over the 21 days to gain possession of the heights, commanding the river valley.*

**October 22nd** A few of the chaps went sick with frost bitten feet.
Orders to the firing line tonight for an attack tomorrow.

**October 23th** The battle of Ancre heights.
It has been a very rough night, raining and cold as charity.

Moved up during the night in the rain, to the east of Les Beoufs. The morning broke with a heavy fog and light drizzle.
We are told that the attack starts at 11am.
At 10.30am we had to re-time the attack to 2.30pm because of the fog.
The fog was clearing well by 1pm and our guns kept up a bombardment on the enemy position.
At 2pm our aircraft arrived overhead and our signallers were in communication with them.
We mounted the parapet at 2.30pm and started to advance towards our objective, which was an enemy stronghold and a machine gun emplacement.
Our artillery opened a splendid barrage of rapid fire, at the same time
We gained our objective at dusk after some very stiff hand to hand fighting.
Casualties were high through inflated fire, caused by the Rifle Brigade, on our left, being held up for about thirty minutes.
We have lost all our officers except eight, but are holding our position without much difficulty.
Reinforcements will have to be sent up as soon as possible.
Some of the Huns put up their hands in surrender, our chap went over to fetch them in. One of them threw a grenade at him, killing him on the spot.
Seeing this, one of our Sergeants gave the word to charge and we bayoneted every one of them.
I believe our losses are one hundred and six.

**October 24th** We were to be relieved last night but no-one came up.
It has been raining in torrents, all night and all morning, so we have muddy water up to our knees.

To make things worse the ration party couldn't find us, so we didn't get the rations.
Relieved by the 31st Division at nightfall, then marched ( I mean crawled) back a mile or two.
Stopped on a waste patch until morning.
We made a small fire, and were given some tea.
Our Adjutant gave us some rum. "He's a real good fellow".
Although we were all wet through, we fell asleep in the mud.
We were all fairly done in.

**October 25th** We walked very steady for about three miles to a tented rest camp near Mametz.
Had something to eat, then the Sergeant Major told us to fetch our rum and drink it down.
It seemed a Godsend to get a bit of rest under cover.

**October 26th** We have spent all day cleaning the mud off our clothes and equipment.
Things are getting a bit shipshape.
The Commanding Officer has sent us a note of congratulations on what he terms, our most glorious work.
I might add that we were the only Brigade to take this stronghold. It had been attacked six times previously.

**October 27th** We entrained to Corbie.
I believe we only stay a couple of days.
We are billeted in a French home with the family.
The landlady is very good to us and will do any little thing to make life more pleasant.
We managed to buy a piece of pork and some eggs at three pence each.

**October 28th** Inspection by the General.
In his opinion we are the best Regiment in France and no Regiment on the face of the earth could do better than we had. We had done much more than he was expecting...perhaps he was trying to give us swelled heads!

**October 29th** A pleasant day in the billet and touring around in the village.
Orders to move tomorrow.

**October 30th** Entrained for Airaines and then marched about twenty kilometres to Huppy.
We had to carry our full kit, including a blanket.
It really was a rough march and I don't think anyone could have gone any further.
I think they are trying to kill us marching, as well as fighting.
My feet are like pieces of raw liver.

**October 31st** Had a rest day, after a clean-up.

**1916 November**
**November 1st** In billets at Huppy.
Quiet day and under orders to move tomorrow.

**November 2nd** Marched to Tours in the rain.
We are billeted in a cellar. It's proper fusty.
We have given it a good dig out.
They are trying to get us some straw tomorrow.
It's been raining nearly all day.

We have had fresh meat once this last three weeks. It's really time they let us taste it again. The last we had was the bit of pork that we bought ourselves.
The rations are poor.

**November 3rd** We are told that we are to be here for a rest for some time.
We started off with an inspection of first aid kits and emergency rations.
One of the fools said that he hadn't any biscuits and couldn't get any, so we are on biscuits tomorrow instead of bread.
Vile weather, raining.

**November 4th** We have had a good clean up in the cellar and now have some straw, which has made the place more cosy.

**November 5th** Military training and drill to get us fit again, so they say.
Weather and rations poor.

***The battle of Ancre heights October 23rd*** *: Between Oct 23rd and November 5th the British and Anzac troops attacked to gain the high ground before the onset of winter. By mid-November the British still fought the battle in the sector and finally captured Beaumont-Hamel on the 18th – 19th .The campaign ended in abysmal blizzards and torrential rain. The estimation of the casualties accruing from the battle of the Somme is subject to much controversy owing to the different methods of assessment employed by the German, French and British armies. (ANZAC -Australian and New Zealand Army Corps)*

*The figures given by the British Official histories 1916 shown for Somme:*
*British 419,654 killed or wounded*
*French 194,541 ( which include 8,000 of the 10th army not strictly on the Somme)*
*German 650,000.*

**November 6th** A draft of two hundred and fifty chaps from home have joined us today.
We are still on very poor rations. We have worked it out that, apart from the meat we have been able to buy, we have only had fresh meat for three days in the last five weeks.
The weather is still vile, continuous rain, day and night.

**November 7th and 8th** Routine of training and drill.

**November 9th** A great day for me – it is in the orders that I have a month's leave from the 18th November to 17th December. I'm so happy that I could just swear for joy.

**November 10th** Training and drill to keep us fit.
We are told that the Dublins are leaving our Brigade and joining up with the Irish Brigade.
I don't know what Regiment is coming in their place.

**November 11th to 17th** This last week has been spent in much the same way, day after day.
After a night's sleep in the cellar on our straw beds, we are training after breakfast until dinner time, then drill in the afternoon.
The evening to ourselves.
The cooking, fatigues and sentry duties are on rota.

**November 18th** Left by transport to go on leave and had a good send-off from the chaps.

**1916 December**

**November 19th to December 20th** On leave.

**December 21st** Returning from leave.
I left Birmingham at 11.20am, arriving in London at 2pm. Had a snack, caught the boat train at 4pm and embarked at 8pm. The boat set sail about 10pm.
It was a very rough voyage. About half the fellows were sick. It wasn't half a mess and the weather was freezing cold.

**December 22nd** Spent a few hours in the rest camp at Le Havre and then marched about five miles to a railway station. Entrained at about 10pm to return to our units.

**December 23rd** We have spent the last twenty two hours in the train, the last six hours we only travelled four miles.
We then marched about six miles to our transport lines where we stayed the night.
It's pretty rough here as we can't get anything to eat or drink.

**December 24th** Christmas eve.
Re-joined the Regiment.
We are in support, in some German made dugouts.
Plenty of mud here and the rain is tumbling down.
They shell us every now and then, but they have not done much damage.

**December 25th Christmas day.** The enemy are very quiet but it is raining hard again.

We have been supplied with waders to get about in the mud. Not much like Christmas.
We have just been supplied with three spoonsful of rum and that's the only drink we have been able to get.
The boys are all talking about home and our officer has said that we will have our own Christmas celebrations when we are relieved.

**December 26th** They have been shelling us, all last night and this morning, so they must have moved more artillery here.
It’s still raining-so you can guess how uncomfortable it is.
Half the Regiment have had to go sick with trench feet.
I really don't know what will happen if this weather keeps on much longer.

**December 27th** Moved into first line.
We had to march through sticky mud in waders.
The mud was up to our knees in places so we just had to keep pulling each other out.
We finally reached our trenches near to Sailly-Sallisel and have a dugout just big enough for four of us to sit up in.
It's freezing hard.
At 10pm I had to take over the dump and only fell over five times getting there.

**December 28th** Heavy shelling by the enemy at night.
To our knowledge there are no casualties in this part of the line, at Combles.
We took the trench over from the French and by the number of dead, they must have had a stiff battle.

**December 29th** Many more of the poor chaps have gone sick with trench feet.

In some cases we had to lift them out of their waders.
One of the German's got stuck in the mud in front of D. Company, but for humanity sake they did not shoot him.
He was still struggling to get out at night fall.

**December 30th** It is still raining.
We have had to withdraw from some sentry posts, because the water in the trenches was up to our knees.
If it keeps raining much longer, we shall have to withdraw to our second line.
The waders are good for keeping the legs dry but almost impossible to walk in the slimy mud. The rubber soles just will not grip. I fell over four times into the mud going just a distance of one mile.
Relieved by the 2nd Lincoln's at 6pm.
Walked about five miles back and then by transport lorries to Bray.

**December 31st** We are so covered in mud we have two days to clean everything.
Bray is a poor camp.
You can't even get a drink and there are no stores to buy rations.

# CHAPTER FOUR...1917

## 1917 January

**January 1st** General inspection of everything at 10.30am. We carried twenty nine of the chaps to hospital with trench feet. The conditions in the trench this last time were the roughest we have had.
A draft of a hundred and sixty joined us this morning.

**January 2nd** We have had a rest day and the weather is improving.
We all paid three pence and went to a picture show in camp.
It was good under the circumstances.
I believe that we get our Christmas dinner next Sunday.

**January 3rd** We are doing military training to get the new hands in trim.
They are trying to get us some beer, so we can open a canteen.
It has been the meeting of mascots today.
The Transport drivers have a rabbit, the Cooks have a cat and we have a small poodle.
They all chum up together, quite a nice family.

**January 4th** A fine day with many of aeroplanes about.
They managed to get two small barrels of beer, which lasted us about an hour.

**January 5th** Inspection by the Corps Commander this morning. Usual speech about very good Regiment.
The Germans set fire to one of our observation balloons, with a shrapnel shell.

**January 6th** It rained in the night and went very much colder as we had a sharp frost in the day.
Our Colonel has been awarded the D.S.O. but we can't imagine why!

**January 7th** Christmas dinner today.
The canteen was open from 11.30am-12.30pm.
For dinner : Roast mutton, Brussels sprouts, carrots, potatoes and plenty of Christmas pudding to follow.
The canteen opened again in the evening and we were allowed a dixie of beer between six of us.
We had a really good day that ended with "Lady" getting a bit tiddly. He fell down and went to sleep.

**January 8th** Went to see a football match but our team lost 4-3, after extra time.
It was a really exciting match.
It has been raining hard again and the mud is back up to your boot tops.
The rum ration has been stopped today, as so many are going sick with a touch of dysentery.

**January 9th** We have been out in the drizzling rain doing parade drill and mending roads.
We don't think that this easy life will last much longer.

**January 10th** Very heavy hailstorms today.
There has been a heavy artillery bombardment on our right for this last three days, but we all reckon the weather is far too bad for an attack.

**January 11th** Snowing quite hard and it is making it even worse to move about.

The artillery horses can't even pull the empty limbers due to the mud.
The Brigadier General has been recalled and we think it's because of the Household Battalion having to go into the line without waders and losing some of the Lewis guns in the mud. They are a lot of moaners.

**January 12th** Snow and rain.
We shall soon be flooded out, if this weather keeps on.
The Regiment has been out all day, making roads.

**January 13th** The Germans shelled a place called Bray, which is just behind us.
They seem to have done some damage with about twenty killed or wounded.

**January 14th** We are still out on road making party.
We went to the pictures last night.
There was a hard frost in the night.

**January 15th** Sleet and rain again.
We move tomorrow to relieve the French somewhere in the line. The Germans have been shelling here again today, but very slight damage.

**January 16th** Marched to a camp near Suzanne and arrived at 6pm, to stay the night.
The roads were very bad and the last transport didn't get here until 11.30pm.

**January 17th** On parade, to march to the trenches at 3.45pm.
It was a really rough march, snowing most of the time and we had over eight hours of it.

We reached our position. It took us nearly two hours to find a dugout in the reserve trenches at P.C. Madame, which is west of Bouchavesnes.
We got settled in by 2am and then at 3am Ginger and I were sent out to guide in the ammunition party.
We are both foot sore and frozen to the marrow.

**January 18th** Snowing and freezing cold.
The French have left this part of the line in a most filthy and disgusting state.
They are a lot of dirty devils, leaving their own muck everywhere. The Germans have got a lot more guns up here than us.
We had a good strafing off them today.

**January 19th** Under heavy artillery, night and day.
Our guns have had a terrible time trying to get up here, but at last they are getting into action.
The transport can't get up on account of the severe weather.
There has been no water issued for the last forty eight hours, so we are gathering snow and melting it down.
It is amazing how much you need to get enough water to make tea.
D. Company have been sent off to strengthen the Household Battalion.
They have many men sick, including the Colonel, Adjutant and the second in command.
They are a poor lot with very few real soldiers. Our chaps are ashamed to be part of them.

**January 20th** Still freezing, it is bitter cold.
The Huns have been strafing us with heavy shells, all day and night.

One of their aeroplanes came over the trenches and started firing at us. We retaliated but he managed to get away.
No water sent up today, so the snow melting game goes on.
We heard that a Staff Captain of the 11th Brigade was killed during the night.

**January 21st** Moved into the first line during the night.
There's plenty of artillery strafing us, all day and night.
We had three killed and seven wounded.
Enemy aeroplanes doing what they like.
Very cold.

**January 22nd** We have some water about two miles away.
As it is rationed we decided it is easier to keep melting the snow, than to try and bring it up.
Two German aircraft have been flying over our lines all day.

**January 23rd** Still freezing.
Our Colonel sent a message to headquarters about the enemy aeroplanes having us under constant observation, during the day. About an hour afterwards a group of French scouting aeroplanes arrived.
We watched as a real aerial duel started. The German plane fell in flames behind our lines.
The men must have been burnt to death.

**January 24th** We got relieved today, to go in reserve.
We have to march sixteen kilometres.
Seven of us from the Regimental Police, were sent back at midday to Brigade headquarters.
As the Battalion will be coming back tonight in the dark, we have to guide them in.
We eventually re-joined the Regiment at 4am.

We were frozen through and I had icicles on my moustache.

**January 25th** Marched back about ten kilometres to a camp at Suzanne.
We are in wooden huts that are awfully draughty, so we don't know whether to be in or out to be warmest.
No water until night time.
Got some tea about 10pm.

**January 26th** A squad of German aeroplanes bombed the camp last night, which did a lot of damage.
We were lucky to only have three chaps slightly wounded, but the "Jocks" had five and a lot of horses killed.
I don't know what happened at the other camps.
It is still bitterly cold.
Daily we have had fifty or sixty going sick with frostbite.
We shall be glad when the weather changes.

**January 27th and 28th** Busy on digging parades.
Our new draft are not a patch on the original chaps. They go sick for the slightest thing and have no pride.
Ginger reckons that they are a disgrace to the Regiment.

**January 29th** Still freezing hard.
The German aeroplanes attempted another bombing attack, last night.
They were driven off by our own aeroplanes, before any damage was done.

**January 30th and 31st** We are still on a so called rest, doing digging and general working party duties.
The weather is still cold.
It has been trying to snow but it is freezing too hard.

We are getting short bread rations.
Rations are now chestnuts or figs instead of jam, but we are getting bacon most days for breakfast, so it is not too bad.
All leave is cancelled again.

**1917 February**

**February 1st** During the night our aircraft brought down a German plane and the pilot is in our hospital.
He says that he did not know it was a camp, he was under the impression that he was bombing a railhead.
It's still freezing hard, far too cold for any more snow.

**February 2nd** Moved to Suzanne in reserve trenches.
A German plane bombed this place the other night killing eighteen horses.
We have no fuel issued, so we have to go out scouting for wood or anything else that will burn to keep ourselves warm.

**February 3rd** German aeroplanes came over during the night, to bomb our lines, but were driven off by our scouts before doing any damage.
Still bitterly cold.

**February 4th and 5th** Still in reserve and very cold.
We spend a lot of time on the scout for wood.
Sometimes get issued chestnuts, in lieu of vegetables which are so scarce out here.

**February 6th** The Germans made an attack on our 6th and 8th Battalions.
Some of the enemy actually managed to get in our trenches, but they did not get out alive.

The attack lasted about five hours, but it was failure for the Huns. They did not gain an inch of ground.

**February 7th** Still freezing hard.
We have been out in the night chopping down some trees, to get wood but the frost has got into it.
It causes the fire to smoke horribly.
It makes our eyes that sore we can hardly see out of them.

**February 8th and 9th** Still very cold over the past few days.
There have been many cases of frostbite.
We now have orders to wash our feet in warm water using a prepared soap, then to dry them quickly and cover them with a type of prepared chalk.
The doctor is hopeful that this will improve our resistance to frost bitten feet.

**February 10th** A Lewis gunner's Corporal was tried today for shooting some wild duck.
He pleaded that he was having some revolver practice. He got a severely reprimand.
We are to relieve the Lancs tonight, on the right of Combles (North of Bouchavesnes).
Relief completed by 10pm, under great difficulty because we had to carry forty eight hour rations.

**February 11th** This is a very isolated forward position.
We can only get in the firing line by night, as there is no communication trench.
The enemy snipers are very active.
A very dangerous place for shells.
We had one chap killed by a sniper today.

**February 12th** Our artillery put down a heavy bombardment during the day for about four hours.
When darkness fell the enemy started a heavy bombardment on our trenches.
We have had one man killed and six wounded.
Very short of water, so we went scouting for some.
We found a well but it was empty.
Still a very hard frost.

**February 13th** Fritz started a heavy bombardment at 5am, which lasted about an hour.
We expected an attack to follow, but nothing happened until 3pm when the enemy artillery started again.
Three enemy aircraft came over to observe our positions.
One was shot down by our scouts and the others retired.

**February 14th** The weather is still freezing hard and we are short of water.
Under a heavy artillery attack during the afternoon, they are trying to blow our front lines in.
Only had one chap killed and two wounded.

**February 15th** Our artillery have been very busy.
It's slightly warmer today and the sky looks hopeful.
The enemy managed to hit a French aircraft with one of their shells which blew up in the air.
No hope for the pilot or observer.
Still hard to get water.

**February 16th** Heavy artillery shelling again today.
The Huns hit one of our sap heads, wounding two men and burying four.

We have been trying to get at them this last eight hours but there are tons and tons of earth on top of them. There is not the least doubt that the poor chaps are dead.
The Irish fusiliers, on our left, had a dugout smashed in, killing four men and wounding two.
A German aeroplane bombed an ammunition depot at Plateau. The explosion was heard miles away.
I believe a lot of damage was done.
We got relieved at 10pm, to go in reserve.
Every one of us will be glad to get back a bit as it has been a very rough time in the front line.
It has been thawing all day, so you can guess there is plenty of mud about.

**February 17th** Came back to the reserve trenches, near Maurepas during the night.
Plenty of mud as expected.
Trenches held by the Rifle Brigade were raided by the Hun, who captured the Lewis gun and six gunners.
No attempt was made by the Household Brigade to help the Rifle Brigade. The result was a free fight between the R.B.'s and H.B.'s.
The H.B.'s are the shakiest lot we have ever had in the Brigade.
I expect that the General will come to sort it out.

**February 18th** Thawing and a lot of rain.
Heavy artillery fire on both sides.
Our chaps that got buried in the sap the other day are being left there and a cross erected.
It would be impossible to get their bodies out.

**February 19th and 20th** Raining on and off during the last two days.
It's so dark at night that you are lucky to find your way back, when fetching rations.
Two of the Rifle Brigade ration party lagged behind and got stuck in the mud.
A search party found them the next morning, unharmed but worn out.

**February 21st** Due to move to a camp, on general reserve.
Marched to the camp which is about ten kilometres at Chipilly. (this side of Corbie).
The whole place is just one sea of mud and we are very short of water.
Rations are poor, no bacon, fresh meat or vegetables.
Some of the chaps went out to try and get a drink and had to step through muddy water all the way.
They came back dead sober and covered in mud.

**February 22nd to 26th** Still in reserve at the "mud patch."

**February 27th** Good weather today, sunshine even for an hour or two.
A most interesting day because we are very close to one of our large aerodromes. We see all sorts of different aeroplanes, some of them are new types.
There is a plane with three wings they call a triplane, which climbs like a rocket.
The triplane is a single seater fighter with a machine gun firing forwards.
Some of the pilots put on a splendid display of aerial acrobatics for us.

**February 28th** Too rough for any flying today.
We are at twenty four hours readiness to move off.

**1917 March**
**March 1st and 2nd** Two good days of weather but it is a terrible place for mud.
A chap got stuck in the mud that firmly, they had to dig him out.

**March 3rd** The Royal Irish Fusiliers played the R.A.M.C. (Royal Army Medical Corps) in the final for the Lambton Football Cup. Some of the chaps were marched there but Porky Preston said that he knew a short cut. I went with him and it was a typical Porky effort. We went miles out of the way and arrived at about half time.
The R.A.M.C. won 3-1

**March 4th** We are starting a four day march to go back for a rest.
We marched ten kilometres to Corbie.
It seems just wonderful to be amongst civilisation again.
We have been buying eggs at three and half pence each and living well.

**March 5th** Marched twenty one kilometres to Villers-Bocage.
It snowed very hard last night, which was why the march was so hard.
I think everyone feels fairly done in.
We got here about 5pm and managed to buy some coffee, but had to have it without sugar.

**March 6th** Marched about twelve kilometres to Beauval, which is quite a big town.
They won't sell us any bread because it is so scarce.
My legs are stiff and my feet are sore but there are a lot worse off than me.
Weather very cold.

**March 7th** Marched about fourteen kilometres to Mezerolles.
One of the chaps has measles so we are in isolation in this village and we may be for some time.
Eggs are very cheap here, two pence each.

**March 8th** Wintry weather, snowing all day.
We are billeted in a barn near to a farmhouse.
The snow is blowing in everywhere and we shall soon have as much inside as there is outside.
Today we had some fresh meat, a first for a long time.

**March 9th** Snowing again today.
The seven cocks in the farmyard started crowing at 2am and woke us all up.
We had tins of sardines in lieu of fresh meat.
The price of eggs has risen two and halfpence.

**March 10th** Weather much milder with a little rain in the night. We heard someone meddling at the barn entrance and "Lady" Hill kept shouting "Come in".
At last he went to see who it was and found out it was just an old cock flapping his wings against the door.
We have not had a change of shirt or underclothing for at least two months.

**March 11th** It is a beautiful morning, the sun is shining, a treat. "Ye Gods and little fishes" we have had an issue of flour. Our cook has made us a jam roll. It tasted all U.K. (meaning like home.)
I don't know what the after effects will be like.

**March 12th** Very cold rain.
Our rest has been cut very short.
We are leaving tomorrow, for a two day march, going nearer the line by Arras.

**March 13th** Marched about nineteen kilometres.
It's been raining all night so the road was in a bad state.
The transport had a rough time. They got stuck in the mud two or three times.
We are at a village, called Rebreuve.
There is plenty of beer, but no money.

**March 14th** Marched about twenty kilometres to Savy, which is about two kilometres from Aubigny en Artois.
It was a very hard march in bad conditions and about thirty of the chaps fell out exhausted.
We are billeted in tents. It is very cold especially in the ones which has no boards, because the ground is very wet.

**Billeted in tents.**

**March 15th** The weather is much improved but most of us are suffering from the effects of those three days on the march.
It took me a good time to get my boots on. My feet have swollen so big.
We have got to find some working parties from our Regiment for work near the front line. "Not much rest this"

**March 16th** We are having trouble with the rations.
Bread is very short.
Even the local French people cannot get anywhere near as much as they need.
We had a breakfast of hard biscuits and jam.
Got paid yesterday so I shall go out to get eggs and with luck, a piece of fresh meat.

**March 17th** Very stormy at times with plenty of rain.
One of pilots lost control, in the storm and flew straight into the ground.
The poor chap was killed outright.
All the Cavalry that was sent to the Infantry Regiments, have been recalled back to the Cavalry. We sent about forty.

**March 18th 19th 20th** We are finding working parties and doing special training.
So I expect we shall soon be doing some more stiff work.
A Regiment of conscientious objectors has come near this camp. They have come out as a working Regiment, looking as much like soldiers as our cat. Nearly all of them looked sick.
If ever the Germans were to see them, they would die of laughter. It is a disgrace to let them wear Khaki.
Our doctor said that if a shell burst within a mile of them they would all die of shell-shock.
They don't half get their legs pulled.

**March 21st** Rain and snow today and blowing a gale.
I think winter is coming back.
Can't get vegetables for love nor money.
Sudden orders to move to Camblain-Chatelain, which is about twenty kilometres away.
I have been left behind, until the 23rd, to guide the men and horses up to the Regiment.
The worst part is I shall not get rations now but they have left me a tin of biscuits, some bully beef and beans. I have a couple of shillings, so I shall not starve.

**March 22nd** Snowing heavily last night.
I could not sleep for rats. The place is swarming.
I was just getting to sleep nicely when some of the bounders started running around my head.
I lit a candle and had a read, then covered my head and got to sleep about 2am.
I gave a Frenchwoman some tins of beans for bread, tea and sugar.

**March 23rd** Marched twenty kilometres with the men and horses to the Regiment at Camblain-Chatelain.
This is a decent village. Most of the men are miners.
The beer is only a penny a glass.

**March 24th** Went over to Marles to see if I could find my old pal, Jimmy Jenks in the 15th Battalion.
I found him without too much trouble.
Jimmy is now a full Corporal.
We saw his company officer and he let him off parade.
Had a great night together, plenty of champagne and other drinks.
It seems a treat to meet an old pal.
I don't know how I got back, I was nearly tiddly.

**March 25th** The weather is still bad, but it is a really good village.
The beer is plentiful and cheap and the civilians treat us very well.
They have a piano in the pub.
If you put a penny in, you get a tune. The boys start dancing with the locals and it all helps to make a bit of fun.
The rations are getting very poor and we have no tobacco because the supply train was blown up.

**March 26th to 29th** The weather is still wintry.
For four days we have been busy doing some strict training for another big push.

**March 30th** The chaps have christened this place "Charlie Chaplin", but it is the best village we have been in for ages.
The only trouble here is that that the food is so short.
We cannot get vegetables.

Sometimes we get oranges and figs in lieu of jam and bread.

**March 31st** Jim Jenks found his way here today and we had a good time in the village. He is just the same old Jim.
Jim has heard that they are moving up to the line, the day after tomorrow.
I expect we shan't be far behind.

**1917 April**
**April 1st** We had a full Battalion parade today and practised new modes of attack ready for the big offensive.
We were out all day and must have covered about sixteen miles.

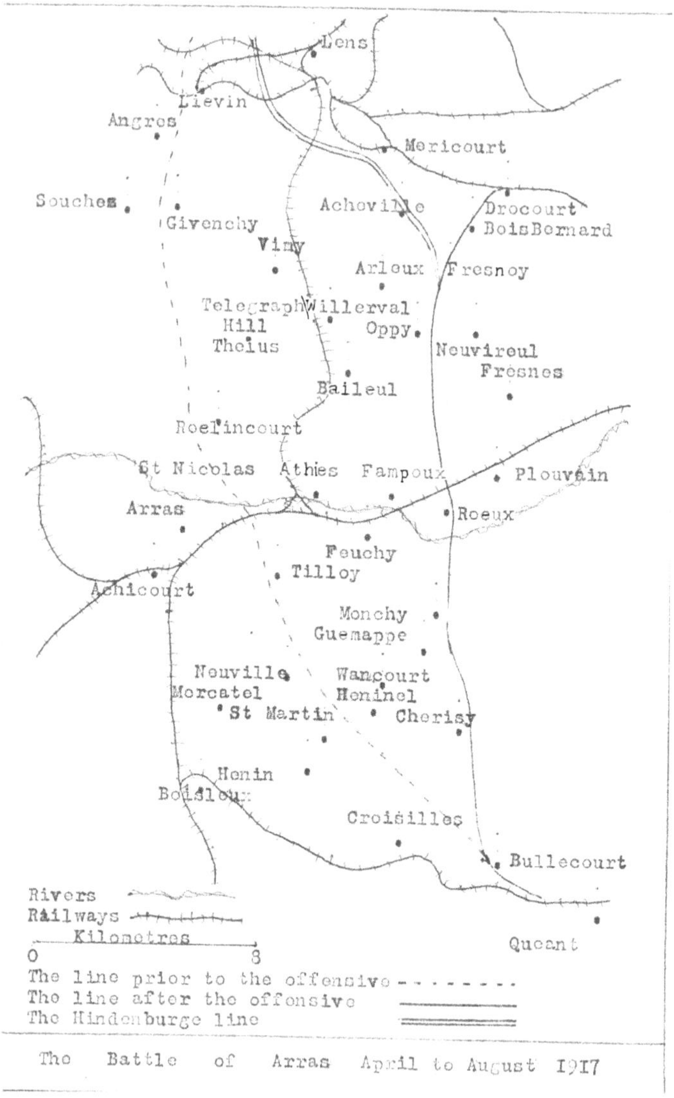


**Map 4. Apr 1917**

**April 2nd** Heavy snowstorms and colder today.
Our 15th and 16th Battalions have moved, closer up to Vimy Ridge where we all expect the offensive to be.
Bill Golby found a new-laid egg and put it in his trouser pocket. He forgot about it until morning, when he put his hand in his pocket and found it smashed up. Oh! What a mess!

***1917 April – Official Report Arras sector.***

***Prelude to the battle of Arras***

*Following the German retreat from the Somme salient they had shortened their line by some 40 miles. This coupled with the Russian Revolution set free a large army of reserves capable of mounting an attack on any vulnerable point on the Western front. After considering alternatives the final allied plan was to attack on two fronts and so to draw these reserves into a defensive, rather than an attacking role. The French with British support were to mount an offensive towards Lacon. The British and Canadian troops were to mount an offensive in the Arras sector to secure the high ground overlooking the Artois county. Vimy ridge was the first objective to deprive the enemy of its observation points overlooking Douai and beyond. The whole of the high ground was heavily fortified , so elaborate plans were laid. Extensive mining and tunnelling to shelter 25,000 reserve troops in Arras, Royal flying Corps action on 5th to 7th April prior to the attack to destroy all observation balloons, bomb the ammunition dumps and to engage the German fighters so that the British aircraft could spot for artillery. This co-ordinated action was carried out in appalling weather conditions and the objectives achieved for the loss of 28 aircraft.*
*The British attack was on a 15 mile front just south of Givenchy – en- Gohelle, south to Croisilles. The Canadians on their left were to be given pride of place in the assault. The 15 miles*

*took in the fortified Hindenburg and the elaborate German triple trench defensive system, some 2 to 5 miles in depth.*

***Official Report: Battle of Arras.***

*The attack opened with an initial artillery bombardment of the defence system, carried out by some 1,000 guns on a 12 mile front. The infantry moved in behind the shell fire and in 40 minutes had captured the whole of the trench first line, with the exception of the strong point Hill 145 at the Northern end of Vimy ridge. The infantry were followed in rapid movement by the machine gunners, trench mortars and other support ready for the second phase of the attack, which followed 2 hours later and met strong opposition mainly at the railway intersection just south of Scarpe river. The attack was halted to enable the artillery and support to move up and with the exception of the railway triangle intersection near Athies, all objectives had been taken. This one holding point proved a great obstacle for the artillery to attack the wire on the 3rd line. However, at midday the advance was continued. The Scottish troops captured the railway junction at 2 pm after bitter fighting. The English troops followed up through the Scots and South Africans attacking north of the Scarpe and took Fampoux. Further north the Canadians with an English Brigade had cleared the Vimy ridge except for Hill 145, which was still held by the German troops. By the end of the first day much ground had been gained and 9,000 prisoners taken. On April 10th the gains were enlarged, the Canadians taking Hill 145. On the 11th the British were reinforced and continued to mount the attack at Bullecourt, but elsewhere German reinforcements made further progress difficult and the artillery had not been able to bring their guns up until the 12th owing to the state of the ground. French Divisions were brought in on the 12th and the attack continued to secure the remaining high ground and the German 3rd line.*

*The first objective had been secured. The German counter attacks had failed.*
*The week's fighting had pushed part of the line 4 miles east, taken 13,000 prisoners, 200 big guns and the heavily fortified defences leaving the German troops with little shelter.*
*A counter attack was made at 4.30 am. on the 15th April on a small sector of the British held front-line was broken through but was repulsed by 1.30 pm leaving 1,700 dead and 350 prisoners taken.*
*The next day a pause was ordered to organise a co-ordinated attack and to try to recover the state of the roads, which has collapsed because of the thaw.*

**April 3rd** Snow storms at night, which turned to rain this afternoon.
Our supply train has been burned up again.
This is the second time in a week. I should think there is some underhand work.
Two small drafts from home joined us today, to make our strength up.
What a time to join the Regiment just before a big do.

**April 4th** Windy and slight rain.
We have just been told that America has declared war. I don't know how true it is.
Scotty has been making some new mixture with soup, jam and biscuits.
Mac had toasted bread with jam on it, his favourite dish.

**April 5th 6th 7th** Marched about sixteen kilometres in a snowstorm to Bethouart where we stayed all night.

**April 8th** Marched to X-camp south of Ecoivres, near Arras.
A long march and we arrived at 10pm.
Orders to move at 6.45am, tomorrow and we are issued with a forty eight hour emergency ration of bully beef and biscuits.
The battle must be near.
The weather is terrible, snow and very cold.

**The Battle of Arras**

**April 9th** At about 5am our artillery opened up a very heavy bombardment.
It was cold and raining and our Regiment was in reserve at St. Nicholas, near Arras.
The infantry started to advance at 5.30am.
The fighting was all in our favour and the Army Corps took nearly three thousand prisoners.
Officers taken prisoner said that they were taken completely by surprise.
The initial advance was about four miles and we consolidated our position in front of Fampoux.
The Germans used a lot of gas shells, but our casualties were quite light, considering the number of troops employed.
The tanks have done some very good work, but the aeroplanes could not do much due to the poor weather.

**April 10th** Heavy snowfalls in the night and we just held our positions.
I expect they are all waiting for the heavy guns to come up closer. The German 2nd line have some very deep dugouts, lit by electric lights with chairs and tables.
The enemy kit bags were full of curtains, clothing, lace and other things looted from the poor people in the villages.

***Official Narrative of Operations, April 11th 1917 Ref. Map Arras 1:10,000***

*The Battalion consisting of 3 Coy's assembled at 1.55 am on the sunken road in support to the Royal Irish Fusiliers. The R.I.F. advanced from their assembly area at 12 noon (Zero). As my Battalion had to pass the first objective at zero plus 40 minutes, I ordered them to leave the sunken road area by zero plus 10 minutes and advance in support of the R.I.F. 2 Coy's in front line 1 Coy carrying. They immediately came under heavy machine gun fire but continued to advance till they found the R.I.F. held up by M.G. Fire. The left Coy then became mixed up with the R.I.F. as it was impossible to advance further owing to the heavy machine gun fire from the Station, Chemical works and Railway Embankment. I gave orders to consolidate the trench. 2 Officers and a few men of the right Coy advanced to within 100 yards of the Station but owing to machine gun fire had to fall back to H18 d2 ½ where the road crosses the railway. They attached themselves to some of the 12th Brigade who were holding a trench there.*

*During the night I re-organised the Battalion in Huddle with the R.I.F. on my right and the Household Battalion on my left. I consider that the failure of the attack was partly due to the fact that we were in view of the enemy practically the whole way from the 4th German trenches to the assembly area, also to the enemy aeroplanes which flew over the sunken road at about 1,000 feet just before zero hour. The enemy put a heavy artillery barrage on the assembly area about 10 minutes after zero, which caused a good many casualties especially to the carrying Coy.*

*G.H. Lacom Major.*
*1st R.W. Regt.*
*14/4/17.*

**April 11th** Cold and windy but dry.
We started to attack from Fampoux at midday.
The enemy have received strong reinforcements.
The village in front of us was alive with machine guns, which were deadly.
We could only advance a short way.
Our support column was caught in heavy artillery fire.
It was a hell of a day, four out of eight of my mates were wounded and my water bottle was smashed by shrapnel.
My haversack got hit but I didn't get a scratch.
We feel very lucky to be alive.
We dug in at night in a heavy snowstorm, wet through.
I feel completely worn out.
We must keep awake as they will very likely attack sometime tonight.

**April 12th** Consolidating our positions.
Heavy artillery bombardment at about 5pm.
The 9th Division mounted an attack, but the enemy machine gun fire was far too strong, and the attack failed.
Our Brigadier General was killed by a shell, today.
The Regiment casualties for yesterday were two hundred and sixty.

**April 13th** Relieved from the firing line for a break.
We are now in the reserve lines, but are under heavy shelling.
The enemy are now using gas shells.

**April 14th** Heavy artillery bombardment by both sides.
The cavalry came up today but had no chance to get into action.
A mixture of rain and some snow today.
We are on hard rations of bully beef and biscuits

**April 15th** Weather still bad and we are held in the reserve trenches.
Orders to move to the firing line tonight.

**April 16th** Marched to the firing line in the pitch black dark and went the wrong way.
We got in at 1am, soaking wet.
It was hailing all the time.
This is a rough part, as they are shelling continually night and day.

**April 17th and 18th** We held the line just to the left of Fampoux.
B. Company had to evacuate their part of the trench tonight.
Enemy shelling has caused it to fall in and four of them were killed and twelve wounded.

**April 19th** Still getting it hot with shells.
It was 5.00am before the ration party came up with our rations.
They could not get through the shelling.
We are getting what they call iron rations, bully beef and biscuits.

**April 20th** Weather dry but cold.
We are to be relieved by the Lincoln's tonight.
As we are still under heavy shellfire our nerves are beginning to feel the strain.
Two killed and two wounded getting out when relieved.

**April 21st** Marched to a tented camp, just outside Arras, at St. Nicholas and stayed for the remainder of the night. Our 11th Battalion came here today, on their way to the fighting line. We marched to the transport lines at 3.30pm.We had to wait about in the freezing cold for motor lorries until 8pm to take us back for a rest, at Beaufort, about ten miles away.

**April 22nd** We are stopping in a barn with plenty of rats for companions.
This is a very quiet village but you cannot buy any bread, even if you have a pocket full of money.
Weather dry but still quite cold.

**April 23rd** Moved to a camp, at Ambrines, where we were joined by a draft of seventy from home.
I believe we stop here to get reorganised.
Weather good today.

***The Second battle of the Scarpe: 23 April 1917.***
*The second battle of the Scarpe was launched on 23 April with a limited objective, Arleux, 2 1/2 miles east of Vimy. The battle with much close fighting continued until 23rd April by which time the failure of the first day of the French offensive was known.*
*Total casualties for the month of April*
*79,732 British, Canadian and South African troops wounded or killed. The sickness wastage was about 5% and the total captures 17,952 prisoners and 254 guns.*

**April 24th to 27th** Spent four days doing Battalion training, at Beaufort.
We managed to have a cold water bath and change of underclothes.
First chance we have had for about three weeks.

We are living well and had tinned rabbit and mutton for dinner,
The rabbit came from America.
The only thing we were short of potatoes.
We can buy eggs at two and a half pence each, so get a good tea now and again.

**April 28th** Sudden orders to move.
Paraded at 9am and marched to Y-camp, near Arras.
It was a really lovely day, but a bit warm for marching.
I imagine we are going in for some stiff fighting again.
We expected a rest but it can't be helped.

**April 29th** Stayed the night at Y-camp and marched to our billet, which is a big store shed in Arras.
This must have been a lovely big town but it has been smashed to pieces, by German shellfire.
They took particular spite on the Cathedral and churches.
The weather remains fine and warm.

**April 30th** Orders to parade in battle order at 4.15pm.
We marched to the trenches, just to the left of Fampoux, arriving at 10pm to relieve the Lincoln's.
On the way we had to run in bursts in an attempt to dodge the heavy shellfire.
The Lincoln's had ten of their men killed by shellfire on their way out.

**1917 May**
**May 1st** Weather fine and sunny.
Our artillery opened up a heavy bombardment, at daybreak but one of the batteries was firing short.
We had one killed and seven wounded by our own shellfire.

On ration fatigue at 9pm.
Had just got started when there was heavy bombardment. The Germans had their heaviest shellfire on a field, we happened to be crossing.
We had to run as fast as we could.
Lucky not to get hit.

**May 2nd** Weather fine and warm.
Heavy shelling on both sides night and day.
One B. Company sentry spotted two forms creeping towards him and opened fire, thinking it was a Hun raid.
One shouted in English and they brought them in. One was dead and the other wounded.
They turned out to be from the Lincoln's, who had made an attack four days previously.
Orders to be ready to attack tomorrow morning, probably at daybreak.

**May 3rd**
**(The 3rd Battle of the Scarpe.)**
Our artillery has been shelling heavily all night but at 4am, they laid a terrific barrage.
At 4.15am we went over the parapet and started to advance.
We had the Irish Fusiliers in support and on our right we had the Household Battalion, with the Seaforths in support.
We were under a heavy German artillery barrage.
The enemy were strongly entrenched with many machine guns.
Our advance was held up by machine gunfire from a château on our flank.
We just couldn't understand why our artillery had not blown it up before our attack.

B. Company was sent to scout the enemy position but only two of them returned.
They reported that the château was strongly held with machine guns. Also to the rear, trenches with many troops..
In the afternoon a bombing party of twenty four men were formed up to raid the château.
They must have been spotted by the enemy lookouts and were caught in very heavy fire long before they got there. Only eight of them returned.
Captain Cox with a small party of men managed to advance way in front of everyone else, but have orders to come back after dark. There is no hope of holding their position.
After dark, what was left of the Regiment re-joined the line, but there is no sign of Captain Cox.
We have taken about thirty prisoners but have no idea of our own casualties.
Trying to get the wounded in, but the enemy shelling has made it very difficult.
A raiding party of thirty men made another attempt to bomb the château, but it was a failure – only ten of them got back. The Hun are far too strong for that kind of tactic.

***The Third battle of the Scarpe 3 and 4th May.***
*Sir Douglas Haig was by now aware of the failure of the French offensive and planned to secure a good offensive line at Arras before beginning the forthcoming offensive in Flanders. The attack was to be limited to villages 800 to 1200 yards away. The action for the 1st and 3rd armies was over in 48 hours. The 5th Army continued for 14 days at Bullecourt. The attack opened between the setting of the full moon and sunrise. The 3rd Army advanced some 500 yards on a 1,000 front in the face of severe opposition. The first army gained a narrow strip on its*

*whole front and the Canadians on the left advanced one mile and obtained the objective Fresnoy.*
*The 5th Army in the attack on Bullecourt started the offensive on May 3rd on a narrow front by the Australian Division. They survived fierce opposition and a number of counter attacks and by the 6th May had gained a wedge into the German position some 2,000 yards wide and 550 yards deep. In the 8 days this wedge was widened to 4,000 yards, containing most of the objective and held against counter attack until they consolidated the position.*
*The losses over the 14 days, amounted to some 13,481 killed or wounded Australians.*

**May 4th** Heavy artillery action by both sides.
We have been expecting a counter-attack by the enemy, but it did not take place.
Weather is splendid.

**May 5th** Under heavy shellfire but we have had no serious casualties.
At 9am, a party of us went out for rations but got caught by heavy shellfire and had to run for it.
One chap of the Royal Irish got killed and two wounded.

**May 6th** Have been relieved during the night and are now in support, about three hundred yards behind the first line.
We are in some holes in the railway embankment, but this place is as hot as the front line.
They shell it very frequently.

**May 7th** The Hun put up two observation balloons at daybreak.

They must have spotted us because we came under heavy shellfire by their artillery on the ground.
Three of our aeroplanes went over and forced the balloons down but in the meantime they caused a lot of damage.
We only suffered four wounded but the Royal Irish, a bit higher up, had ten killed and twenty five wounded.
You dare not move in case they spot you and their artillery start shelling.
After dark, four of us went into Fampoux to try to salvage some chairs, tables and other useful things for the officers to work with, but had to get out pretty quickly as the enemy started to shell it.
The village is just a ruin.
There is hardly a building left standing.

**Scale of Destruction.**

**May 8th** The Germans have been shelling very heavy all day.
They put one of our 9.2's out of action.
Our own battery has been forced to move back, after the Hun got the range and shelled them heavily.

Raining all morning, so no aeroplanes about.
We take over the front line tonight.

**May 9th** Very rough day of shelling again, five wounded.
We had a rough passage going for the rations, as we had to run, to get out of the shelling.

**May 10th** We have withdrawn from the front line so that our artillery can shell the Hun front line.
The German line is too close to ours, for our artillery to lay a barrage, while we are still there.
Returned to our position after dark and got shot at by one of the Irish Fusiliers. He thought that we were the enemy.
Our sergeant was slightly wounded.
We thought for one horrible moment that the Hun had taken over our trench.
Had to put out a fire when we were fetching the rations as one of the Huns shells hit our pile of smoke bombs.

**The battle of Arras – Final stages:**
**May 11th and 12th** Orders to prepare to attack later today.
The weather is keeping fine.
Plenty of shelling on both sides.
At 7.30pm our artillery really put on a heavy barrage just behind the Huns first line.
We went over the parapet, straight away.
Got to our objective very quickly where we captured about two hundred prisoners.
Our losses were light considering the advance, we reckon about fifty all told.
Consolidated our position by 3am.
Their artillery have been firing very heavy all night but we have hung on to what we have gained.

At 7am, we started the advance again and took Roux, the cemetery and chemical works.
This place has changed hands no fewer than six times.
We have been the only Division that has been able to carry through our objective.
Captured another three hundred and fifty prisoners.
All very tired and weary but are getting relieved tonight.

**May 13th** Relieved by the 51st Division at about 2am.
We had bad luck on the way out as a shell burst in death valley killing one and wounding nine others.
Stopped at the "Blue" line till 10am and had a cup of tea and some warm soup.
The best meal we have had for the twelve days we have been in action.
Marched to Arras, then had motor lorries to take us about thirty five kilometres to Houvin.
We are here to reorganise and get fit again.
The Divisional General has been chatting to us, congratulating us on our splendid work.
He is as proud as a peacock.

***Official report***
*A series of local actions took place all along the Arras sector to mislead the German High Command into thinking that this was to be the sector of the great advance. Villages were taken, lost, retaken, until 20th May when a large assault was mounted against the Hindenburg position South East of Arras. Local operations continued through July and into August Ground had to be gained to a depth of 5 miles along a 25 mile front.*
*Total casualty figures for the Battalion of Arras;*
*British , including Canadians, Australians, South Africans;*
*29,505 killed, 20,876 missing. 108,279 wounded.*

*Thus was the cost of a diversionary offensive of no strategic importance carried out to engage the German reserves and relieve the pressure from the French offensive.*

**May 14th and 15th** Spent two days having a good clean-up and are enjoying the break.
The weather is quite warm and the rations reasonably good.

**May 16th** The Brigade was inspected by the Corps Commander. The usual talk of how proud he was to command us and how we must feel on our triumphant advance.
Something to remember for the rest of our lives.

**May 17th and 18th** Some rain but nice and warm.
We are busy training to get fit for the next round.
Also having some Brigade sports in a few days' time.
Billeted in a barn as usual.
Water for washing is very scarce.
The French won't give us any, so we have to take it when they are not looking.
Spires found a barrel of something, which he thought was French wine.
We just got our dixies and sampled a drop.
Couldn't tell if it was wine, beer or cider, but it made some of the chaps run pretty smartly to the potty.

**May 19th to 24th** We had some sports for the Regiment.
There was plenty of fun, especially the water carnivals, mop fighting and sack bumping.
Then we had a slice of cake and a few biscuits for tea.
To finish off we had a concert.
A splendid day.

Still continuing our special training, ready for another big push, I expect.
The Commanding Officer and the Adjutant have both gone on a month's leave and some of the men on short ones.
The first leave since January, 1917.
The weather has been splendid.

**May 25th** Decoration parade.
Captain Warren was awarded Military Cross and Lance Corporal Guest a military medal.

***Extract from the 1st Battalion Royal Warwickshire Regiment Diary May 25th 1917***

*A fine day. Battalion paraded with Brigade for presentation of decorations to officers, N.C.O's and men of the Brigade by the Corps Commander XVII Corps*
*Captain D.A. Warren R.A.M.C., attached 1st R.W.R. Military Cross.*
*No. 1266 L/Cpl H Guest "A" Coy 1st R.W.R. Military Medal were presented with ribbons. In a short speech the Corps Commander congratulated the Battalion on having done the finest thing that has been done in this war viz. –*
*Breaking through and keeping 4 lines of German trenches on April 9th .*
*He also remarked upon the excellent operation successfully achieved on the day before the brigade came out of the trenches on 11/12 May when, after being in the trenches for 12 days, they took the chemical works and Cemetery.*
*He paid tribute to the memory of Brig General Cosling and Captain Fellows (Brigade Major) who were both killed during the recent operations.*
*The Battalion carried on training after the parade as per program.*

*G.H Lacom Major*
*Commanding 1st Btn RWR.*

4th Division Training Programme.

| Date | Div | Time | Training | Place | Remarks |
|---|---|---|---|---|---|
| 03/06/17 | F | 10.00 am | Church Parade 10th Infantry Brigade | Map 51C | D Coy on range |
| | I | 11.00 am | Inspection of Coy's and billets by | 1/40,000 | |
| | R | | Commanding. Officer | H.13 b.5.1 | |
| 04/06/17 | S | 6.45-7.45 am, | Running drill | | |
| | T | 8.45-12.30pm | Open Warfare Platoons in attack patrolling Use of ground etc. | Vicinity of billets Beaufort area. | A Coy on Range |
| | | 2.30-3.30 pm | Map reading | H.13 b. 5.1 | |
| 05/06/17 | B. | 6.45-7.45 am | Inspection by O.C. Coy's | Billets | |
| | T | 8.45-12.30 | Route March Magnicourt - Sars Les Bois | | |
| | N | | Berlancourt-Entree Wamin-Houvigneul | | |
| | R | 2.30-3.30 | Feet inspection & lecture by Coy Cmdr. | | |
| | O | | On consolidation and Strong Points | Billets | |
| 06/06/17 | Y | 6.45-7.45 am | Box Respirator drill | Near Billets | |
| | A | 8.45-12.30pm | Section & Platoon drill. Musketry drill | | |
| | L | | Rifle exercises. Bayonet fighting etc. | H.13 b 5.1 | B&C Coy |
| | W | 2.30-3.30 | Lectures by Coy Cmdr on aeroplanes | | |
| | A | | Map reading & Intelligence Reports | | |
| 07/06/17 | R | 6.45-7.45 am | Physical Training | H.13 b 5.1 | D Coy on range |
| | W | 8.45-12.30pm | Fire Orders | | |
| | I | | Recognition & Description of Targets. | | |
| | C | | Judging Distance. | | |
| | K | | Rapid loading and Firing | Beaufort area | |
| | S | 2.30-3.30 pm | Physical Training | H.13 b 5.1 | |
| 08/06/17 | H | 6.45-7.45 am | Running Drill | | |
| | I | 8.45-12.30pm | Route March by Coy's combined with | Road to | |
| | R | | teaching | Ignaucourt | |
| | E | | Use of ground and method of siting and | | |
| | R | | dealing of Strong points | | |
| | E | 2.30-3.30 pm | Musketry Drills | | |
| 09/06/17 | G | 6.45-7.45 am | Box Respirator drill | | |
| | I | 8.45-12.30pm | Platoon & Coy drill. Rapid loading & | Near billets | |
| | M | | Firing | H.13 b 5.1 | |
| | E | | Musketry Drills | | |
| | N | 2.30-3.30 pm | Inspection on Drill field of kits, Ammunition, | | Backward men |
| | T | | Respirators and Smoke helmets | Ditto. | On range under |
| | | | | | Musketry officer |

Physical Training, Musketry Drills, Bombing, Bayonet fighting, Dummy grenade throwing, N.C.O.'s under Adjutant R.S.M. from 2.30 to 3.30 on Mo We Fr Men not actually firing

belonging to Coy's on range, carry out Drill as per programme.

G.H. Lacom Major commanding 1st Btn RWR.

**Bayonet drill**

**Gas mask drill.**

**May 26th** Today was sports day and a great day it has been. The sports day started at 2pm and our Regiment won the overall trophy "The General's Shield".

We had seventy one points and the nearest to us were the Royal Irish Fusiliers, who had forty six points.
The General was very happy about it, being an old Warwickshire man himself.

**May 27th 28th 29th** The weather has been good.
We have been busy with the usual training routine.

**May 30th** We handed in our winter blankets today so I expect the weather to change tomorrow.
The 12th Brigade had their sports day, today and the mile was open to all comers.
Corporal Sheppard from our Regiment won it very easily, by fifty yards.
Have just heard that my old chum Jimmy Jenks was wounded in the leg by shrapnel, during the last battle, and spent three days in a shell-hole before they could get him in.
Very pleased to know that he is now off the danger list and on his way to hospital in England.

**1917 June**
**May 31st to June 9th** Routine training, drill and kit cleaning.

**June 10th** A terrific storm about 10pm, it kept up all night.
It was one of the worst that I have ever witnessed in my life.
Talk about the roar of the guns that was nothing near it.
Expecting to go into action any time.
We mustn't grumble because we have had a really good rest this time.

**June 11th** Orders to move tomorrow, so the usual kit inspections and last minute parades.

**June 12th** Left Houvin at 2.30pm and marched about a mile and a half.
We were then taken by motor lorries, to Arras, arriving at about 6pm.
Are being held in reserve here, staying in a cellar.
Seven killed by shellfire and one or two wounded on our first day back.

**June 13th** Still in reserve in our cellar in Arras.

**June 14th** Plenty of aircraft about here today.
The Germans generally get a hot reception when they come here.
About 8pm four planes came over flying low, firing at the troops in the street.
The enemy must have captured them, as they had British markings.
No one took any notice of them, until they opened fire.
Our own pilots soon realised what was happening and shot them down.
Sergeant Williams got the Distinguished Conduct Medal.

**June 15th** The Germans have been shelling us today, with long range guns but we suffered no casualties.
There is a cinema here, so I went today to see the pictures.
It was a fairly good show.

**June 16th** Still in reserve and the weather is good.

**June 17th** Heavy shelling this morning, a few more houses knocked down and eight of the Seaforths wounded.

We moved at 2.30pm to Blancy wood, to be closer up in reserve. It is splendid water here.
A hot day and the spring water is as cold as ice.
We can also have a dip in the river when everything is quiet.

**June 18th** Thunderstorms today and the weather is very muggy.

**June 19th** Rainstorms but very hot.
We left here at 8pm, for the firing line.
Got there about 10.30.
Golby, and I went back to meet the ration limbers, to guide them to the ration dump.
We finished this duty at 2am and the night was so hot that we were wringing wet with sweat.

**June 20th** Raining today.
Both sides are very quiet.
Towards night the aircraft got busy, so both sides started shelling.

**June 21st** Heavy shelling night and day.
We had three killed and five wounded.
Among them was Sergeant Williams who had the D.C.M. a few days ago and was due for leave.
That's really hard luck.

**June 22nd** Our artillery bombarded the Huns heavily about 10pm for about half an hour and then one of our planes dived down, machine gunning their firing line.
A very risky performance and I'm sure the enemy expected an attack after it.
Got relieved about midnight.

We are behind the firing line, at Stirling camp, in support of the Irish.

**June 23rd, 24th and 25th** Still behind the lines in support but still under shellfire.
Luckily no one hit.
The weather is splendid.

**June 26th** Moved up to the forward trenches, in support.
We had to do this in small groups, because Fritz has a lot of observation balloons up.
We have been making one or two small raids just to keep them busy.

**June 27th** Very hot with rain storms.
I was on gas sentry duty during the night and at about midnight the Hun started sending a few gas shells over.
Making up my mind, whether it was serious enough to raise the alarm, when it just poured down with rain and put an end to his little game.
We have to keep very much on the alert when the wind is in his favour.

**June 28th** Rain on and off all day.
The Canadians on our left made an attack at about 7pm.
I believe they gained all the ground, asked for.

**June 29th** The Hun was busy last night bombarding pretty well all night.
They also sent over a few gas shells.
Very little damage done.

**June 30th** Rain again.
Some shelling on both sides, but very little damage just here.
No casualties.

**1917 July**

**July 1st** Moved up to the front line during the night.
It's been another wet day and our artillery had been strafing the Hun trenches.
I expect they will be strafing our trenches now.

**July 2nd** Heavy enemy shelling during the night.
Quiet during the day and then started again as we set off to bring in the rations at 10pm.
I had the misfortune to break my false teeth.
They just came to half when I was washing them.
I wonder how I will get on now.

**July 3rd** Both sides engaged in artillery attacks.
We had one hit our trench, killing two and wounding three.
It's a bit too hot for our liking here, at the moment.
Just don't seem to be gaining anything.
It's been raining, day and night so plenty of mud again.

**July 4th** Terrific bombardment by our artillery at 2.30am, which was to allow some of the 12th Division on our right to attack. From all reports it seems that they didn't do well against all the extra guns that the enemy has brought up.

**July 5th** Relieved at about 12.30am and went into reserve, behind our lines at Dingwall camp.
We were lucky in deciding to go the main road way out and had very little difficulty.

The machine gunners went along the canal and had two wounded by shellfire.
Got settled in and had some sardines with our rations – they made a nice change.

**July 6th** We got settled down to sleep about 2am.
Had a good rest until about 10am.
We were cold, as we have no blankets and our overcoats haven't come up yet.

**July 7th** Went over to St. Laurent Blangy at 7.00am to have a bath and change of underclothes.
I really felt a lot better for it.
Weather is very good.
We had a bit of fresh meat today but it was not enough for all of us so we tossed up with the Signallers and we lost.
Just our luck.
Got some more sardines though.

**July 8th 9th 10th** In reserve and splendid weather.
Fairly quiet here, but Fritz shells us now and then.
He isn't doing much damage.
They have started shelling Arras again today.
Recently both sides have started aerial bombing attacks, on camps behind the line, where troops are resting.
We have done a spot of digging in case it happens here and came across a number of French soldiers just under the ground, so we gave them a proper burial and erected a cross to "Unknown French Soldiers".

**July 11th** Private Coleman is on Field Court Martial for refusing to go out on a working party to the trenches.
We reckon that he will get twelve months.

Headquarters played C. Company at football and we won 6-0.

**July 12th** Just as we expected an enemy aeroplane bombed us at 3am, but not one casualty and little damage done.
Weather still fine and warm.
Our overcoats arrived today!

**July 13th** Went to the dentist in Arras.
He can't do my teeth at once, but will mend them and send them by post.
I shall find it awkward being without them.

**July 14th** Weather unsettled.
We are getting some rainstorms.
Whenever it starts raining both sides start shelling.
I think they do it to make life more unpleasant for us chaps.
Had two rabbits between ten men as rations today – You could put both of them in a cup.

**July 15th** Fritz has been shelling Arras again.
I don't know what damage they do, but I do know there are a lot of French civilians, who have come back there to live.

**July 16th** Went in support to the firing line and are in dugouts on the railway cutting but it is none too safe.
Two men got wounded before we had been here five minutes.
Fritz shells this place, day and night.
Rain and stormy.

**Carnage.**

**July 17th** Heavy shelling again.
One of our limbers had a direct hit, killing both the horses, but the driver was lucky as he had just left them for a moment.

**July 18th** Weather is good again but Fritz is very busy with his aeroplanes.
They tried shelling this position all night but were off target.

**July 19th** Working hard building up this position, so it looks as though we are holding this place for a time.
Not so much artillery activity today.

**July 20th** Still working strengthening the position.
I was sent for by the Adjutant this afternoon, who asked me if I would care to go down to the country for a fourteen days' rest.
Of course I jumped at the opportunity and thanked him very much.

**July 21st** Left the firing line at 9.30am to report to the transport and get instructions regarding the rest camp.
I am in charge of our party of five.

**July 22nd and 23rd** Left Arras station at 10pm in trucks.
Arrived on the 23rd at St. Valery at 8am.
We marched about two miles to the camp, where we had breakfast.
Saint Valery looks a splendid village.

**1917 August**

**July 24th to August 4th** This has been a grand summer holiday.
We are having a real rest away from it all.
Each day we rise at 6.30am, draw rations at 7.00am and then breakfast at 8.00am.
The mornings we spend in keeping the camp clean and tidy and then we have our dinner at 1pm.
We have each drawn one pound pay, which has to last the fortnight – it's not much but we haven't let our lack of funds spoil our enjoyment.
After dinner we are free to do anything we please and we can go anywhere, providing we are back for roll call at 9.00pm.
Our afternoons have been spent just like a holiday at home, walking on the beach and getting crabs and cockles, playing cricket, football or tennis and strolling around the village.
For the first seven days the weather was really grand and even when it changed to rain, the officers in charge here did their very best to make it enjoyable for us.
When it was wet, we had afternoon concerts in the YMCA hut given by Martin Harvey and Lena Ashwell's company.
It was really good entertainment and are most grateful to them for coming out here.
The evenings we have spent at the whist drive or the cinema, which only cost three pence.

Sometimes we go out into the village for our tea or supper, but had to cut down as our money started to run out.

**August 5th** Left at 11.30am to re-join the regiment.
We reached there about 11pm to find them in reserve, near Blangy.

**August 6th** The Regiment in reserve camp are training hard for the Division sports, to be held tomorrow.
I heard that the Irish Fusiliers have left us to join the Ulster Division.
A Battalion of the Middlesex will replace them.

**August 7th** It's the day of the sports and we have orders to march to the firing line.
We were able to watch most of the sporting events before preparing to move off.
By that time the Regiment had won all the running events.
A great day for the Warwicks.
Moved off at 7.00pm and arrived in the trenches about 9.00pm
The enemy were quiet so we had no difficulty getting in.

**August 8th** The enemy started a heavy artillery barrage at about 3.30am.
Which they followed up with an attack on the trenches to our right, held by the Notts and Derby Regiment.
Their attack failed and two of the Huns were captured.
The enemy had many wounded or killed, for the loss of seven of our chaps wounded.

**August 9th** Very bad weather again and in places we are up to our knees in water and mud.

The Division on our far right, who are covering Monchy, made an attack at 7pm, helped by our aeroplanes, machine gunning the enemy from a low level.
We can't find out how successful the attack has been.

**August 10th** We are beginning to think that the strain is sending some of our officers slightly mad.
One of them from the Manchesters took a party out to reconnoitre in broad daylight – needless to say that he got killed and four of his men wounded.
One of our balloons broke loose and went sailing right over the enemy lines. Our anti-aircraft guns opened up but they couldn't hit it.

**August 11th** Cloudy but dry.
Four of our aeroplanes attacked eight of the enemy.
The odds were too great and one of ours was forced down behind the enemy lines.
It seemed to us that his engine was hit.
We go in support of the Middlesex, who are relieving us tonight. It's their first time in the firing line so we shall have to keep our eyes open and help them as much as we can.

**August 12th** Raining on and off all day. I was on gas sentry duty today. I have been issued with a rattle, in addition to the Strombos horn.
Orders are : For gas shells we use the rattle, for gas clouds we use the horn.
The rattle is a big thing, like the ones they use at the fair, so I can hardly stop myself from giving it a few swings and shouting out "Come and try your luck, Sir!"

**August 13th** Raining again and of course the mud is getting worse.
The enemy have been fairly quiet, little shelling and no gas.

**August 14th** Another fairly quiet day.
We have been busy on the dugouts, trying to make things a bit more comfortable.
The trench is busy filling up with mud, so it's a job that we can keep at all the time.

**August 15th** The enemy are heavily bombarding a position, to our left, which we think must be Loos.
It's been fairly quiet in our position again today.

**August 16th** Our artillery are in action again, over by Loos, with a very heavy and sustained attack.
I expect that the Canadians will attempt an advance.
We came under an artillery attack this afternoon.
The enemy hit one of the dugouts, wounding five of B. Company. Weather is awful. Just rain, rain and rain.

**August 17th** Enemy very quiet but plenty of aeroplanes about.
We expect to go out on a small bombing raid, when it gets dark.
Fritz has been busy last night, putting out extra wire.
It looks about 10 ft. high, so we have abandoned the idea for a time.

**August 18th** Much artillery and aeroplane activity on both sides. The aeroplanes have been out spotting for the artillery on both sides.
The scouts have been busy trying to keep them away.
Got relieved from the line tonight, to go in reserve.

**August 19th** Got a letter from my old peace time chum, Percy Kelsey this morning.
He has moved up here, so I will try and meet him 6pm at Arras station.
I met Percy and he was looking fine.
When we found a quiet place, we had plenty to tell each other over a few bottles of champagne.
I was quite tipsy by the end of the evening, as it was quite some time since I had had a real drink.

**August 20th to 23rd** Still in reserve.
The weather over the last three days has been much better.
Plenty of sunshine but very rough wind.
Our second battalion are only about ten miles away.
A lot of them came here to see old friends.
We played their team at football. They beat us 2 -1.

**August 24th** Some rain again today.
A digging party was sent out to the village at Blangy.
They were asked to dig up money and valuables, buried there by the French, when they moved out.
The French police and some of the villagers were there.
Our chaps dug up over six thousand francs, some of the villager's jewellery and valuables.
The grateful !!! French collected it all in and gave our chaps five francs to share between them.

**August 25th** Kit cleaning, arms inspection, with some military training in the morning.
Bath at the candle factory, St Nicholas.

**August 26th** Orders back to the firing line. We marched from here at 7pm and arrived at about 9pm.
We were wringing wet through, the rain just didn't stop at all.
So wet that we couldn't sleep.

**August 27th** Went out on ration party, in the early morning.
It was a very dark and wet trip.
We got another good soaking, while waiting for the limbers to come up.
The soil here is very chalky, making it almost as slippery as ice.
We were sliding all over the place coming back with the rations.

**August 28th to 30th** Three days of rain.
The conditions are very bad for moving about, but it has made operations very quiet on both sides.

**August 31st** A company was sent out on a reconnoitre party in the night.
They came back with an enemy machine gun and ammunition, which they found in a shell-hole, in front of the trenches.
The weather has improved, so the artillery have been active again.

**1917 September**

**September 1st** Weather is very stormy.
Holland, has been trying his hand at cooking.
He's been soaking biscuits, boiling them and then mixing them with a tin of jam.
It looks a real mess but it was all eaten up.
We all reckon he deserves a Cook's Military medal.
Scotty swears he tried to kill him, with his so-called jam pudding.

**September 2nd** We organised a night raid to try to capture a machine gun that has been causing us a lot of trouble.
The moon was shining too bright to attempt it, so we will have try for it later.
The Sergeant cook sent us some bread dough down as a special treat, but it was as heavy as lead.
I only had a little bit of it but even then it was chasing round in my tummy all day. (Don't want to break my teeth again.!)

**September 3rd** The Seaforths relieved us about 10pm.
We have been very fortunate this time in the trenches, only three of the chaps wounded in the eight days.
Arrived at our billets at midnight, to be told that we are to be on the move again in a few days' time.

**September 4th** Had a clean-up and change of underclothes and went into Arras, to meet Percy again at 6.00pm.
We had a few drinks and bought some tomatoes for one franc, but the bag burst, so I arrived back a few short.

**September 5th** A general clean up and kit inspection.
We are on orders to move tomorrow, but don't know why or where.

**September 6th** We started on the march at 1.00pm.
It was very warm and muggy and seven of the chaps dropped out before the first halt.
They were overcome by the weight of their packs and the heat.
At the second halt, at Achicourt, we had rations and a full hour's rest, which refreshed us all.
The next stage was completed without incident and then we had a heavy rainstorm.

Continued in the rain but got so wet that it was running out of our trousers.
We eventually arrived at the village of Bailleval at 6.30pm and all felt worn out.

**September 7th** We are told that we are here for special battle training, for the next big push.
A draft of two hundred, from home, joined us.
We are led to believe that most of them are conscientious objectors.
They will get more fighting than they bargain for, if they try anything funny on the chaps.

***Special Divisional Order 4th Division 9th September1917.***
*During the three months that the Division has been holding the line in the Scarpe Valley much work has been demanded of all ranks, in order to improve the defences. The line taken over by the Division in June had only recently been wrestled from the enemy and consisted of a front line with a few supporting trenches, mostly in a poor state of repair: That handed over in September was a completely organised line, with a continuous Support and reserve trenches and good dugout accommodation for the Garrison. In addition much useful work has been done in the improvement of camps and communication in the back area.*
*That such a result has been attained in spite of considerable difficulties from bad weather is a testimony to the hearty co-operation and good spirit shown by all ranks in pushing forward the work and is most creditable to all.*

*I feel sure that the same spirit will be shown in the forthcoming training and that all ranks will do their utmost to fit themselves for battle, during the short time available.*
*W. Lambton.*
*Major General commanding*
*4th Division.*

**September 8th to 15th** Regular routine of drills, special military training and route marches to keep us fit.
In the afternoons we are managing to get in some sport.
Our Company have won the Colonel's prize for football.
He gave each man ten francs.
General Lambton fell off his horse and is injured.

**September 16th** Routine as before and today the Regiment got into the second round of the Brigadier General's Cup, by beating the "Jocks", 1-0.
It was really a good game, exciting all the way through.

**September 17th** Fine but windy weather for the Cup final.
Our team played Brigade Headquarters.
Extra time was played, twenty minutes each way, but still no score.
The replay is at 4pm tomorrow.

**September 18th** A fine bright day. The Cup Final was played as planned and the Regiment beat Brigade headquarters 3-0.
There was as much excitement here as there is for the Cup Final at home.
In the evening we had a concert and it was A1.
We have a pro, in our Regiment, who played the page in the sketch "The Lady and the Page".

Our running match scheduled for today has had to be cancelled, on account of us having to move tomorrow night. Barney Clifford hurt himself in a fall.

**September 19th** Marched away at 6.15pm and arrived at the railhead about 8.00pm.
Had rations and entrained in trucks leaving at about 11pm.
Arrived at Proven in Belgium, at 7am, so we are not very far from Ypres.
We then marched to a nearby camp for a bit of final training.

**September 20th** We are at a farm near Proven and our billet is in a barn with no sides.
The people of the farm have to keep a cow in here with us at night, because it is poorly.
Tiddly Watson has it as a bed chum as he sleeps near her.
We have to be careful here because Fritz bombs this camp at night.

**September 21st** Fairly good weather today.
We have been expecting our pay this last few days but the cashier won't arrive until tomorrow, about 8.30pm.
A German aeroplane was knocking about somewhere near camp, so we had orders to put all lights out.
Some of our planes went up, then the searchlights got to work, so he was picked off quickly.

**September 22nd and 23rd** Two days of lovely weather and special training.
We have to be careful here, as Fritz is bombing this place every day and night.
Fifteen people were killed in Poperinge yesterday.

**September 24th** Good weather continues.
The Seaforths had their sports day today and we did quite well in the open events.
We are living all right here, as we are able to buy us some vegetables.
Sometimes we go weeks without any, as they are difficult to get. Barney Clifford is still in hospital with his fractured rib.

**September 25th** Our Division's General Lambton fell off his horse a few days ago and fractured his collar bone.
Our new General, named Malcolm, inspected us in full battle order today.
I expect we shall be on the move soon, up towards the firing line. Weather very good.

**September 26th** Played the Middlesex Regiment at football and won 4-0. They were quite downhearted.
Orders to move up tomorrow.

**September 27th** Marched from camp at 10am and entrained at midday to Elverdinge near Ypres.
Marched to a camp at Breary.
We are stopping here, in reserve. (There is a train line to Vlamertinghe from which they could have marched to Brielen )

**September 28th** This is one of the hottest camps we have ever been in.
Last night there was a full moon and a procession of German planes went over the camp.
They were dropping bombs, from about 8pm, until about 2am.
Some damage to the camp itself and some casualties in the Middlesex Regiment.

**September 29th** German bombers over again in the night at the same time, in the bright moonlight.
Some bombs were dropped on the camp.
A good deal of damage with more casualties again – this time among the horses.
Good weather and fairly quiet during the day.

**September 30th** Another night of hellish bombing.
In the last three nights the Middlesex Regiment has had fifty casualties.
We have had six wounded and the poor horses.

**1917 October**

**October 1st** Fritz was over again bombing.
Three of them were picked out, by the searchlights, but the anti-aircraft gunners couldn't hit them.
Two of our H.Q. chaps wounded.
Weather very good for October.

**October 2nd** We go up tomorrow night, to try and force the enemy out of their present position.
Bombing planes over again.
Four of our Regiment got hit.
Daddy Watkins, on Head-quarter's duty, is in a serious condition.

**October 3rd** Sorry to say, poor Daddy Watkins died early this morning, another of the old boys gone.
It's been raining today.

At 8.15am we left for the front line, carrying full order, bombs, rifle grenades, extra ammunition, forty eight hours ration, and three sandbags.
We also have either pick or shovel. We could hardly get along.

**The battle of Broodseinde.**
**October 4th** The early morning started with dirty miserable cold rain.
The cold seems to go right through you.
The artillery opened the attack at 6.00am and it seemed as if hell was let loose.
At the same time the infantry started their attack.
The Seaforth and the Middlesex were in the first wave.
We formed the second wave and H-battery was in reserve.
The attack is on a eight mile front.
On our left is the 29th Division and on our right the 11th Brigade. The attack was one of the hottest that we have ever been in from the start.
We beat the enemy at every point before 7am.
After an hours break, at this position, we then started for our final objectives.
This proved to be very hard fighting.
Heavy casualties were suffered by the Seaforths and Middlesex but we succeeded in forcing the enemy back and reached the position at 12.00 midday.
At 1pm, the enemy started a counter attack but was held back twice, by the Seaforths.
The enemy regrouped and at 3pm launched a fierce attack, forcing the Seaforths and Middlesex regiments back.
We were sent in to try and retake the position and after an hour of heavy fighting Fritz tried another counter-attack but we held them easily.

The line we hold is just shell-holes. We are working hard to make them as strong as we can for defences.
It's a bitter cold night with occasional rain.

**October 5th** The German aeroplanes have been out at first light to find out just how far our advance has reached.
Their artillery has been shelling us all night, but so far all the shells has fallen way behind us.
The prisoners captured on all fronts yesterday amounted to some four thousand men.
Our Regiments casualties were one hundred and fourteen killed, wounded or missing.
Two of our aircraft collided in mid-air and they plummeted into the ground. The crews must have been killed outright.

***October 4th The Battle of Broodseinde.***
*This battle was the last of the three stages of the Plumer plan to secure Gheluvelt Plateau. The first stage was the battle of Menin Road bridge (20 to 25th September).*
*The second, the battle of Polygon wood (26th September) is the final stage to put the allies on the top of the Ypres ridge. The Northern flank was allocated to the British with the Australians and New Zealanders forming the centre of the main attack around Broodseinde – in their honour the battle was so named. The following day the King sent the following telegram to Sir Douglas Haig "The continued success of my gallant troops in Flanders gives me the highest satisfaction and reflects great credit both upon your leadership and the efficiency, courage and*
*endurance of all ranks concerned,"*
*George R.I. 5th October 1917.*

***Sir Douglas Haig - dispatch.*** *"Our line has now been established, along the main ridge for 9,000 yards, from our starting point near Mount Sorrel. From the furthest point reached the well-marked Gravenstafel spur, offered a defensible feature along which our line could be bent back from the ridge."*

**October 6th** Very cold, rough winds and heavy hailstorms.
All the wounded have been evacuated and we are making the position as strong as possible.
To be relieved tonight.
Golby and I were sent back early to find the resting place, so that we can guide the Regiment in later.
The camp is just a field with some bivouacs put up.
When the Regiment came down it was 6.30am before they were all in.
We are all done in, as we have not been able to get a sleep this last three nights.

**October 7th** Slept all day until teatime.
We then had some food and a double rum ration about 7pm.
Got down to sleep until morning.
The camp staff tells us that it's rained all day.

**October 8th** It's raining very heavily.
The Colonel has told us how pleased the High Command is, for what he called our splendid work.
We have to go up the line to Jolly farm, again tonight.
He said it is rather rough on us, but we shall get a rest next time out.

**October 9th** The Regiment started about midnight to return to the line.
I find that I am one of a party of six men ordered to take tea up to the men on the light railway.
At 1am we loaded the truck, then started on our journey.
All went well for about two miles and then the trouble began.
The track-line has been under shellfire and the truck came off the lines about five times in the next mile.
We also had to wade through water, a foot deep, in places pulling the truck.
Then about a quarter of a mile ahead Fritz started heavy shellfire smashing the track-line up for a good distance.
That did it!
We just sat down soaking wet on what was left of the track and sent a couple of chaps off to get a carrying party to get the stuff in.
After guarding it for just about an hour the party arrived. Fritz was shelling like mad and we finally reached the Regiment at about 4.30am, without a single casualty.
Been lucky again but what a hell of a night.
The weather is terrible.
Raining and hailing all the time.
The mud in places is over a foot deep.
We are in reserve to our 12th Brigade who are making an attack today.

**Mini Railway.**

**October 10th** Still raining.
The 12th Brigade did not capture all their objectives, but have held their new position.
We have to relieve them in the firing line tonight.

**October 11th** Moved up in the night to relieve the 12th Brigade and had a terrible time.
It was such a pitch black dark night that we just couldn't see where we were going.
The going was so difficult, with the mud and shell-holes, that we were lucky to get in before daylight.
The enemy were shelling constantly but we had only three casualties.
The line is just composed of a shell-holes and there is at least a foot of water in the bottom.
Just heard that the Household Battalion that went up with us got caught in a heavy barrage and had over forty six men dead or wounded.

***1917 October 12th** **<u>The First battle of Passchendale.</u>***

*Official report. : The greatest effect on the battle was made by the complete break in the weather, causing the ground to be most unsuitable for a rapid advance. Progress depended upon construction and maintenance of lines of communication across water filled craters, streams and mud. Crown Prince Rupert wrote in his diary for that day : "Rain, our best ally"*

*The attack was launched between the Ypres – Roulers railway and Houthulst forest. The renewed attack made some headway along the spurs and high ground, but in the valleys below the swollen streams had flooded and the advancing troops plunged nearly waist high in mud. Many were lost in the darkness and were rescued with difficulty.*

*The advance in the valleys were forcibly cancelled, but on the higher ground it continued and further North the Guards and English County Divisions gained their objectives in spite of the appalling conditions and eventually communications were restored and the gains consolidated.*

*Note : the second battle of Passchendale took place between 26th October and 10th November with the Canadian Corps and guarded on the left by 4 divisions of the 5th Army. The advance was confined to two narrow causeways between bogs and streams. The village of Passchendale being taken on the 6th and more of the ridge on the 10th. At this stage Sir Douglas Haig closed the campaign for the winter to proceed with the battle of Cambrai.*

**October 12th (The First Battle of Passchendale.)**
Very wretched morning with drizzling rain.
The artillery opened their barrage at 5.20am and at the same time the Household Battalion and ourselves started the attack.
We reached our objectives after about an hour and a half fighting but it was one of the toughest jobs we have ever had.
You could hardly drag your feet out of the mud.
If the enemy had been any good at all he ought to have held us back easily, but they started to retire as we got to too near.
We are determined to hold our position until we are relieved tonight.
No idea of our casualties but are sure that a lot of the wounded will die through the effect of the mud in their wounds.

**October 13th** Another very dark night and we did not get relieved until nearly daybreak.
The guides bringing up our relief got lost in the blackness and went past us.
It was so dark that one of the companies ended up at a German post and brought back two prisoners.
By the time it was all sorted out, it was too light for us to attempt to get out of the line, so we must stay here another day.
Everyone is wet through to the skin. It's cruel luck.

**October 14th** Got out of the firing line without any losses in the early morning.
Three of the chaps and myself went on a stores party, to bring stores from Jolly farm down to the canal bank.
We had a real game of it.
The truck kept running off the rails.
Over in the mud would go the whole lot.

We did not get to the Regiment until 12.30pm, soaked to the skin and worn out.
At 1pm a fleet of twelve enemy Gotha bombers, escorted by thirty scouts started to drop bombs on the troops.
It was a really lively ten minutes, lucky for us they just missed our camp.
Some of the other camps are a terrible sight.
There must have been at least one hundred casualties besides the poor horses.
Some of the Big Chiefs at home ought to have been here and then perhaps they would want some reprisals.
At 1.30pm we marched to Elverdinge and entrained for Proven.
We reached Proven about 4.30pm, then marched to a camp, about three miles off.
Some of the poor chaps had to be carried, as the rough time had been too much for them.
What with the weather and the mud it has been one of the roughest offensives that this Regiment has been in.
The whole Division has done grand.
In the two attacks we suffered some two hundred and fifty casualties.
It really turned out far better than we expected, considering what a hell-hole this whole district is.

**October 15th** The Germans made another aeroplane raid last night, but they did not touch our camp.
Marched to K camp near Poperinge.
We were joined by one hundred and eighty Cavalry, but I expect they will be with us just for the winter months.
Our Colonel, Sir C.M. Lacom gave a splendid speech on behalf of the General Staff, thanking us for the extra good work of the Battalion. I believe, from what he said, that he is one of the proudest men in the world today.

**October 16th** After a good night's sleep we spent the day getting our kit into some sort of order.
We're preparing to move off again tomorrow.

**October 17th** Paraded at 4.00am, then marched to Poperinge. We entrained at 7.30am for Aubigny, which we reached at 4.30pm. Marched to Y-camp, which is some eight kilometres from Arras. At Etrun we settled in at about 8pm.
Scotty was on duty at Hazebrouck, to patrol the platform to prevent the troops from getting onto the station, but the train set off without warning and he got left there.
He had the luck to join up with the "Jocks" and arrived about four hours later.
We were all very pleased when we got bread issued, as we have been on bully beef and biscuits for the last fortnight.
Weather cold but reasonably dry.

**October 18th** Had a really good clean-up today and we are very glad to get down south again, for a bit of a break from the bombing and shelling.
Some of the Cavalry chaps have not had leave for eighteen months so I expect I will have to wait for mine for a few more weeks.

**October 19th to 22nd** We have had four days of routine training getting the Cavalry draft prepared for trench work. The weather has been cold and we have had some rain.

***To all ranks of the 4th Division***

*Nobody will ever forget the part taken by the 4th Division in the GREAT BATTLE OF FLANDERS 1917.*

*In eight days you have had three fights in the most trying conditions that any troops have had to endure, and in the words of the Army Commander "the performance was marvellous". The demands made on the artillery have surpassed all previous records and the gallantry and determination of the Infantry have been beyond all praise.*

*Machine Gun Coy's, and Light Trench Mortars Batteries have materially assisted the Infantry and in spite of heavy losses have shown the finest throughout.*

*As usual the gallantry of the linesmen and devotion to duty of all members of the Signal Service have been splendid. But for the unceasing energies of the Royal Engineers and Pioneers the movement across country and the transport of material up to the front would have made the operation impossible.*

*Last but not least a great debt of gratitude is due to the R.A.M.C. personnel with the attached Infantry Stretcher Bearers for their never ceasing efforts to bring in the wounded and save them from unnecessary suffering. Nobody could be more proud than I of commanding such troops.*

*I thank and congratulate you all. 13 October 1917. T.G. Matheson, Major General, Commanding IV Division.*

***The following message has been received from the General Officer Commanding Fifth Army.***

*During the short time that you have been under my command, you have fought magnificently. You have had to contend not only with desperate resistance on the part of the enemy, but also with rain and mud equally formidable. In spite of this the 4th Division has fought as successfully as it has been done gallantly. I send my best congratulations and my warmest thanks. 18th October 1917. General Gough. Commanding FIFTH ARMY.*

**October 23rd** Moved to Achicourt near Arras and arrived at 6.30pm.
Weather still cold and wet.
Orders to move up to the reserve trenches tomorrow.

**October 24th** Very rough night and arrived all tired and wet at about 8pm.
We are in the reserve trenches, on our right is Monchy.
It is fairly quiet here and like heaven after the Ypres attacks.
The 12th Division have been holding this position and Percy Kelsey is in the 12th but I expect they have now moved north.

**October 25th to 31st** We are still in the reserve trenches.
The shelling is not very heavy.
We have had a week of very cold weather with plenty of rain.
Three of our chaps and myself are out on the lookout post, night and day.
We have to write an intelligence report every day, telling what shelling the Germans have done, size of enemy shells, whether they are highly explosive, shrapnel or gas, and the number used. We also log the observation balloon numbers, time up and time down, with the compass bearing from this post.
We also report all hostile aircraft, what direction they are travelling, how far they get over our line and by which means they are driven back.
At night we watch for gas shells or cloud gas and also note the colours being used by the signal flares and any S.O.S. signals.
It keeps us very busy but it is interesting and the time goes quickly.

**Horse Gas Mask.**

**1917 November**

**November 1st and 2nd** Moved up to the 2nd line at 5.30pm. Headquarters and two Companies are in a café, which is really a great big cave.
It was dug out by the French convicts, years ago, to get the stone to build the cathedral at Arras.
The cave has been fitted up with electric lights by the Royal Engineers and it is quite safe from shellfire.

**November 3rd** Misty weather and some rain.
Fritz has been shelling all day.
At 7pm the enemy sent over a lot of gas shells and bombarded the front line with trench mortars and minnies.
Our Regiment had only one casualty caused by the gas, but the casualties of some Regiments was heavy.

**November 4th** One of our chaps at headquarters, named Holland, was accidentally wounded.
A rifle bullet had at some time been dropped near the fire and it exploded, cutting his cheek to the bone just below his eye.
It looks rather serious so I wouldn't be surprised if he is sent home to have it treated.

**November 5th** Moved to the front line in the night and got in without loss.
The trenches are in fairly good trim.

**November 6th** The weather is still unsettled.
The enemy is quite active at night with trench mortars and minenwerfers.
Spent the day between guards working on the dugout.

**November 7th 8th and 9th** It has been raining most of the last forty eight hours and very cold.
The enemy is still active with mortars and minnies.
We got relieved at 6.30pm and proceeded to Arras down the Cambrai road, which was under enemy artillery fire but fortunately nobody was hit.

**November 10th** In camp just outside Arras for special training with hand bombs.
We will be here eight days.
Got to practice for a big bombing raid that we are making somewhere about the 18th.
We are not allowed into Arras, without a pass and they only allow a few men at a time.
It's like being a prisoner.
The Commanding Officer, Sir G. Lacom has been awarded the D.S.O. for **our** good work at Ypres.

**November 11th to 14th** Still on routine training.
I am told that I go on leave on the 15th.
Let's hope that all leave is not cancelled before my turn comes.

**November 15th** Spent the day cleaning up and sorting kit.
Caught the leave train from Arras just before midnight.

**November 16th to 29th** Arrived at Boulogne at 8.30am and sailed at 9am.
A good crossing, arriving in London at 3pm.
I had a snack and caught the 4.40 to New street, arriving at 7.05pm.
On leave from November 16th to 29th .
Stayed at my sister, Polly's house at Yardley.
Had a good time meeting up with my old chums still on the trams. They are either too old or medically unfit for active service.

**November 30th** Left New Street to return from leave at 12.35am and caught the boat train at Victoria at 6.30am.
Boarded the boat at 9.30am but it was a rough sort of crossing and plenty of the fellows were seasick.
Got to Boulogne and stayed at St. Martin's camp .

**1917 December**

**December 1st** Left St. Martin's camp at 9.30am and entrained for Arras, arriving at 7.00pm and stayed the night with the Drums.

**December 2nd** The Germans have been shelling Arras today.
I re-joined our Regiment, who has just come out of the trenches, to be in reserve.
We stop here for eight days.
My company had six men killed during this time.

**December 3rd to 8th** In the last five days we have been doing hard battle training, practising for an attack.
We are under enemy shellfire.
Although it is bitter cold, we are not getting a rum ration.

**December 9th** Raining very heavily all night and day but it is not so cold.
We are afraid that the weather may stop our offensive because there is so much mud about.

**December 10th** We are still in reserve at Wilderness Camp on Arras - Cambrai Rd.
It is a wilderness too.
We can't show any light, as we are under observation from the German lines.
It's bitterly cold again.

**December 11th** From information given by prisoners, the Germans are massing troops in front of our position.
At 5am we had to go to the assembly trenches, to be ready in case the Germans attack.
We stopped there until 9am and then returned to the wilderness. Heavy shelling all day.

**December 12th** All reserve troops again up to the assembly trenches from 5.00am to 9.00am.

The artillery are also standing to with their horses near the guns to limber up at a minute's notice.

**December 13th** Moved up to the chalk pits, near Monchy, at Feuchy-chapel crossroads, so that we are near to the front line in case of emergencies.

**December 14th** A Hun prisoner caught last night tells us that they have massed troops and are on standby from 2am to 8 am, expecting an attack from us.
Orders to move to the trenches tonight.

**December 15th** Moved up to the front line at Monchy, to relieve the Middlesex Regiment.
The enemy are very active and we are under shellfire night and day.

**December 16th** Shelling again very heavy.
The Hun have knocked a section of the trench down where A. Company are stationed.
They were lucky to get away with only seven wounded.
It's still bitterly cold but at least we did get a rum ration.
The first for about a month.

**December 17th** Started snowing today and Fritz is shelling like mad.
One of the old boys of A. Company was killed by a shell.
The enemy has also started sending gas shells.
We have to man this position every morning from 6.00am until 8.30am in case the enemy attack.

**December 18th** Moved our position, a little over to the right, to try to get away from the heavy shelling.
One of our men was killed and two men wounded just as we were about to move.
We fully expect the enemy to attack any minute.

**December 19th** Cold and freezing.
We were under a gas shell attack at 4.00am and most of us got a touch of it.
It burns your throat and causes coughing.
During the day there has been a lot of aerial activity.
Both sides have made heavy artillery attacks.

**December 20th** The enemy is still active and the weather is freezing cold.

**December 21st** Fritz made a bombing raid during the night but the sentry spotted them on the way in.
They came under our rifle and machine gun fire and suffered heavy casualties.
Later in the night we had another gas attack.
Luckily no casualties.

**December 22nd** Moved across, to the position on our left, under heavy shelling.
One of the shells landed in our trench, killing five of the chaps and seriously wounded Sergeant Major Ganby.
They also smashed part of our front line in, by concentrated mortar fire.

**December 23rd** Fairly quiet in the night and its started thawing in the night.
At 6.30am the Germans opened a terrific bombardment on our front line and support trenches, then made an attack on Y-sap. They put up a barrage on the entrance of the sap, making it impossible for the men in the sap to get back to the front line. The Germans then followed up with a raiding party.
Our chaps fought a pitched battle and managed to get the Lewis gun back but two gunners and four bombers are missing, so possibly prisoners.
The bombardment on our position continued and we had three killed and seven wounded with shrapnel.
At 9pm Fritz changed over from shrapnel and high explosive to gas shells and twelve men have been sent back to the hospital suffering from the effects of gas.
So far it has been a lively night.

**December 24th Christmas eve.** The only thing seasonable about it is the hard frost that we had during the night.
Fritz has been shelling us heavily again.
We are having our Christmas dinner on New Year's Eve, by which time we expect to be out of the trenches.

**December 25th Christmas day**. It started to snow very early this morning and has been snowing on and off all day.
We stand to for three hours every morning expecting Fritz to attack.
Christmas fare : We had half a loaf each man and a packet of chocolate. Bacon for breakfast, chocolate for dinner, bread and margarine for tea.
Heavy shelling all day and it's freezing cold.

**December 26th** Freezing very hard and everywhere covered in ice.
The ground is so uneven that it is almost impossible to stand up, we just slide about.
We go in the support line tonight.
It's been one of the roughest sixteen days we have had up front. Not only the bad weather but the heavy shelling has caused us to have had over forty casualties.

**December 27th** It's still bitterly cold and I seem to have felt it more than ever these last few days, but the shelling has eased off a bit today.

**December 28th** Plenty of enemy aircraft about today and one was shot down just behind our line.
The pilot and observer were captured and one of them had a wooden leg.
They must be getting short of airmen.

**December 29th** Weather stays very cold and frosty but the enemy have not been so active.
Orders to be relieved in the night for a four day rest.

**December 30th** Relieved early this morning and marched to a camp near Arras for a four day rest.
Everyone is just about worn out.
We are having our Christmas dinner tomorrow.
Very hard frost again.

**December 31st** Spent the morning having a good clean up of kit and a bath and change of underclothing.
At 1.00pm we went for our Christmas dinner.

Menu : Beef, Pork and vegetables, pudding washed down with a glass of beer, with some nuts and apples to follow but no oranges.
We also had a gift of cigarettes from America.
It was a very nice dinner but very quiet.
On duty from 3pm until 7pm but then went off into Arras for a few drinks.

# CHAPTER FIVE...1918

**1918 January**

**January 1st** New Year's Day.
A bright sunny morning but freezing hard.
Plenty of aircraft about, but Fritz has not shelled the town today.

**January 2nd** A quiet day in camp and a good rest.
Only two hours on Headquarters guard duty.

**January 3rd** Moved up to Foss farm, to be in close support, in the night.
Fritz must have spotted us as we started the move, as we had to try and dodge his artillery fire the last mile.
I really thought my time was up, but we got through with one killed and eleven wounded.

**January 4th** Still freezing.
Every night Fritz sends over some gas shells so we have to be on the alert.
He also shells this place, especially during the night.
We are having it rough as we are doing sixteen, sometimes twenty, days in the trenches and only four days out.

**January 5th and 6th** We are still having it rough, heavy shelling and very cold weather.
That's the trouble with being right up in close reserve – the shelling is almost as bad as being in the firing line.

**January 7th** Moved up to the firing line in the night, the enemy is still very active.
In some places our saps are only thirty yards from the Germans, so we have to be on the lookout all the time.

**January 8th** Still very cold weather, that makes it about five weeks of frost, it will be a novelty to feel warm.
The enemy has been shelling heavily again.
The Hun blew a large hole in our water tank, so now we have to fetch the water from about a mile away.

**January 9th** Just after midnight I was on guard and noticed the thaw was setting in.
I could feel the change in the weather, it was so marked.
By midday the water was rushing down the trench and the whole place was a stream.
It took us all a great deal of hard work to keep the trench intact by stopping it from caving in.
Back to the mud again – I don't know which is worse – the cold or the mud!

**January 10th** Still thawing and showers of rain.
I'm on sentry duty two hours on and four hours off.
When we are off duty, we have to set about getting some of the water and mud out of the trenches before the whole lot collapses in on us.
We are hardly getting any sleep.
Eight men have been sent back to hospital, just too exhausted to carry on.
Fritz has been shelling us again.

**January 11th** The thaw continues and it's raining.
The sides of the trenches are falling in everywhere and the water is running down the trench like a stream.
We work night and day to keep the trench passable.
Left at 4.30pm to go to the second line.
Finally arrived in the pitch dark at 6.30pm, to find the trenches as bad as the ones we have just moved out of.
We found a dugout with only a couple of inches of mud in the bottom but I was so worn out that I flopped down and slept right through until 10.30am, next morning

**January 12th** A day of shovelling water and mud to make the trench habitable.
Most of the dugouts have fallen in but a strong wind had come up and that has helped us a lot.
We have got things shipshape.
It looks as though we are due for a frost tonight.
Fritz has been shelling but much lighter than usual.

**January 13th** Freezing hard in the night and then a really bright day.
Many aeroplanes of both sides about.
Fritz has been shelling, on and off, all day and night but we have not had any one hit.

**January 14th** Started to snow in the early morning.
Orders to keep extra guards posted.
The General staff expect the enemy to make an attack here, so we have to keep a sharp lookout.

**January 15th** Heavy rain all night.
We started to move from the second line to the firing line at 3.30am.

I was detailed to meet a party bringing up gum boots at Foss farm.
The party arrived at 9.30am, by which time I was soaked to the skin.
We reached the firing line at 11am, to find it a "shambles".
The sides are falling in and it is up to our knees in water.
More than half of the rations had to be dumped on the way.
It was impossible for the ration party to get them up through the mud.
Some of the boys had to be helped out as they sank so deep in the mud.

**January 16th** Still raining now and much of the firing line trenches have completely fallen in.
It is impossible to use them so we are just taking a chance on the top.
Fritz must be in the same state because we can see them walking about on their top.
We are getting no sleep as we are working nearly all the time trying to make the trenches passable.

**January 17th** No rain at all today so we are trying to get things a bit straight.
We have had to evacuate some parts of the front line.
It's so deep in mud and water some of the chaps have collapsed through exhaustion and have been sent back.

**January 18th** Just a drop of rain today.
We have been able to build the trenches up a little, but we still have to go over the top to the front line.
Most of the chaps don't seem to care anymore what happens.
The Germans are in the same plight, they can be seen at times walking over the top.

**January 19th** Managed to get some sleep and woke up to a fine bright morning.
Plenty of aeroplanes about.
About 11.30am we watched a combat between two of our aircraft and two Germans.
A good fight ensued, ending in a German plane being brought down.
At 7.30pm, we went back to the second line.
We had to go over the top, because of the state of the trenches, but the enemy was quiet.

**January 20th** Showery.
It has taken me nearly all day to get the mud off my jacket and trousers
They were absolutely lathered up.
Fritz has been rather quiet today.

**January 21st** Went to Tilloy at 7.30am, to get a bath and change of underclothes.
It's been about three weeks since the last bath and change.
Every night we are on a working party up at the first line and get back early in the morning.

**January 22nd** Raining nearly all day and we are back with the mud.
A draft of fifty joined us from home today, most of them are only young chaps.
Orders to go to Arras tomorrow for a four days' rest.

**January 23rd to 26th** Four days of drill and training.
I don't know why they call it a rest.
We can't even go into town without a pass.

Just like being a prisoner.

**January 27th** Moved up to the second line, north of the Arras –Cambrai road.
We were able to get there in the afternoon as there was a thick mist.
We really expected an offensive or something to happen today as it is the Kaiser's birthday. It's been fairly quiet except for the usual shelling.

**January 28th** Freezing hard in the night.
Plenty of shelling on both sides.
The Germans are making plenty of raids on this front.
We think they are trying to judge the strength of our line.

**January 29th** A nice clear night but freezing.
The artillery have been very quiet but the Germans have been aerial bombing around about here.
Spiers mixed his rum with vinegar and kept smacking his lips saying how nice it was.
We tasted it, and it almost made us heave.
Spiers has been busy ratting all night.
He caught one in a wire loop. He went to hit it with a stick, to kill it, but hit the wire instead, which broke and the rat got away. His score to date : six rats caught ( three kills – three escapes). The boys have been pulling his leg all day.

**January 30th** Cold and misty night .
We are doing plenty of work every night, making a lot of strong point and putting plenty of barbed wire out.
Fritz will get a shock if he comes over tonight.
The rations have been fairly good lately, especially when they have to be brought over the top.

We are still unable to use the communicating trench.
At 10pm, a heavy artillery bombardment opened up, followed by an enemy attack on our right.
We were expecting something to happen, so the chaps were waiting and the attack fizzled out.

**January 31st** Moved up to the first line at 6.30pm.
It was misty and pitch dark.
It took us all our time to keep to the right track, as the communication trench was too bad to use.
Enemy fairly quiet in the night, except for a few gas shells.
Plenty of aeroplanes about during the day.

**1918 February**

**February 1st** Sentry duty all night. Two hours on and three hours off.
Weather quite good.
The enemy was quiet until 9pm, then we were bombarded with tear-gas shells.
This gas really makes your eyes smart and water.

**February 2nd** The enemy have been shelling our post today.
We had some very narrow escapes but nothing worse than a good shake up.
We came out to the post in the night over the top and found a pile of dead bodies in a crater.
They must have been there for a few months, as only the bones were left.
Had we been able to use the communication trench, in the usual way, we shouldn't have found them.

**February 3rd** Quiet night and a very bright morning.
A large number of aeroplanes about and we watched a battle between six German and three of ours.
During the battle six planes were brought down, two of them in flames.
By this time the battle had moved a long way from us, so that we do not know which side had two planes left.
We had a spot of luck in the observation post spotting one of Fritz's transports a long way behind his line with a high load of hay, but our artillery didn't go into action.
We have just worked out that it is eight days since we had our boots off.

**February 4th** Fine day but cold.
Fritz has been shelling at intervals all day but we have suffered no casualties.
Relieved at 7.30pm by the Royal Scots, 15th Division.
We got out without any trouble and marched to Arras.

**February 5th to 9th** We have been in Arras for a so called rest. Regular routine of work up the line at night. Digging and strengthening the ditches, putting out more wire and other odd jobs.
The days have been spent, battle training.

**1918 March**

**February 10th-March 4th** We are stopping in Arras for a rest. We were to have gone out of the fighting area but they are afraid Fritz is making a big offensive here, so we kept in reserve.
Plenty of work up the line and very strict training.
Fritz bombs this place every moonlit night.

**March 5th** We had a sudden order to move up the line at 6.00am but when we got there, it was an exercise to see how quickly we could get there.
We got back in Arras at 12 noon.
We have been playing football.
Tomorrow is Cup final day for the Lambton Cup.
We are in the final against the R.A.M.C.

**March 6th** Cup Final day.
A really smashing game which was fought on in extra time and still ended in a draw.
The replay is tomorrow if we are still at "rest" in reserve.
Games played so far : 1st round beat Duke of Wellington's Regt.
2nd round beat Seaforth Highlanders.
3rd round beat Bye
4th round semi-final - beat West Yorks regt.

**March 7th** A splendid day for the replay.
The sun is shining and there is very little wind.
The final kick-off was at 2.30pm.
The excitement was terrific.
A cup-tie at home was nothing to this.
There were thousands of spectators and a lot of them had bugles, gas rattlers, old tins and anything that makes a noise.
The game again ran into extra time and we finally won 2-1.
On the second goal everyone seemed to go mad.
I can't remember a match like it here or at home.
The winning team : Cpl Smart, Pte. Rushby, Tanby Gibson, Lieut. King, Sgt. Young, Pte. Edwards, Pte. Hubbart, Pte. Kingsberry, Pte Horton, Pte Moore, Pte Mountford. Reserve : Watson, Mailly, Evans, Cpl. Bird, Major Willis.

They each received a silver medal.
The Silver cup is a bonny one.

**March 8th and 9th** Regular routine and still hanging on in reserve.
We came second in the Divisional competition, for the best section in Field Firing.

**March 10th** Still hanging on, ready to go into action, any minute. We had a General Officer Commanding's inspection and he expressed his appreciation for the gallant and good work we have done.
He said he knew he could trust us, to carry on in the future.

**March 11th and 12th** Still standing by in reserve.

**March 13th** Breakfast at 4.30am.
We then packed everything up so that we should be ready to move in fighting order.
I think they are expecting Fritz to make an attack any minute.
Everyone had to stand by all day but nothing happened, so we did not have to go into action.

**March 14th** Unpacked everything and stood by.

**March 15th to 18th** Standing by to move but so far all is quiet.

**March 19th** Moved up in the pouring rain closer to the trenches. We are in the reserve line for a few days.
It's been raining all day.
Relieved the A. Regiment of the Grenadier Guards, at the railway triangle in Blangy.

**March 20th** Rain early morning, cleared up to give a nice fine day.
The enemy has been very quiet.
Too quiet for our peace of mind, something must be coming off soon.

**March 21st** Terrific artillery bombardment opened at 3am and kept on until 10am.
High explosive, shrapnel and gas shells were used but our casualties have been very light.
We are wondering about the civilians in Arras, as it has been shelled heavily.
The weather has been grand today. A real spring day.
A fellow of ours died suddenly this morning.
He went to see the doctor but I believe he died before the doctor had seen him.
I think it was the first natural death we have had out here in the line.

**March 22nd** **Ludendorff's German offensive.**
We are still standing to night and day and under heavy shellfire all the time.
The Germans are attacking all along the line.
We have had to evacuate our front position, as our right flank has been driven back.
This is causing inflated artillery fire, in one part of the line.
The enemy sent forty thousand mustard gas shells.
The casualties have been very heavy and all the ground is so poisoned that the chaps are dying like rotten sheep.
Ordered to evacuate as it was impossible to hold the position.
We moved back to our reserve trenches.

**March 23rd** The weather again has been beautiful and spring like.
Very hard going night and day.
The enemy artillery have been trying to blow us out, but so far we are hanging on.
The division on our right have lost Monchy, which is a very high point.
It has left us in a precarious position.
If they don't hold them on our right we shall get nearly encircled. Our guns have moved right back, under cover of darkness, to prevent any chance of them being captured by the Hun.
Once again we think "Save the guns, never mind the infantry".

**March 24th to 27th** We are under constant shelling and Fritz has brought up some very heavy, big guns.
They are trying their best to smash all our fortifications.
The enemy aeroplanes are flying about in large numbers, sometimes swooping down near our trenches and firing their machine guns at us.
We cannot get any sleep as we are expecting another attack.

**March 28th** Fritz started at 3.15am, with one of the worst artillery barrages I have ever known.
Very high explosives and gas shells all mixed up.
At 8.30am the barrage lifted and the enemy attacked all along our lines.
They must have outnumbered us five to one, but we held them until 11am.
The 15th Division on our right was driven back through sheer weight of numbers.
We are told they lost all their officers except two.

Our Colonel, Sir G. Lacom and a few of our officers, seeing how critical the situation was with our right flank, being exposed, rushed over to the 15th division.
They rallied them into a reasonable line.
Thus, giving us a chance to make a good retirement and get back in a position level with them.
Had it not been for the prompt action and gallantry of our Colonel and his officers, we should have been encircled and wiped out. Their aeroplanes were actually coming in at ground level from behind us and strafing the line – we were all very glad their aiming was poor.
We held this line until about 1pm, when we had orders to retire to another position about six hundred yards away.
We fought a very good rear-guard action and the whole line retired, in very good order to the new position.
The action was fought so well that we didn't lose a single gun, not even a machine gun.
The General is delighted, no doubt he thought it was all up.
I shall be glad when I can look in a looking glass to see if my hair has turned grey.

***Ludendorff's Offensive Arras, St. Quentin area, 21st March 1918. The German offensive in Picardie.***

*During the early days of March reports brought back by British aircraft of construction and preparations by the German forces in the area, combined with the evidence of deserters, made it clear, that despite the diversions of attack in other areas the main thrust would be between the Scarpe and Omignon rivers. On the night of* ***20th March*** *the British artillery bombarded the assumed assembly areas and in favourable wind the St. Quentin area was attacked with cloud gas. Just an hour afterwards, at 4.30 am, the Germans opened the offensive with heavy artillery bombardments alternating between attacks on the command posts and the British front line.*

*The attack began in fog (even at sunrise the visibility was only 10 yards) and despite the fact that the British artillery were forced to wear gas masks, making them virtually blind, they remained in action and were still in position at 11 am, when the fog lifted and the foe was at last visible. The German main objective was aimed at securing the bridge heads on the Crozat Canal and the high ground round Cambrai. In all, 64 German Divisions were employed on the first day of this attack. This exceeded the total fighting strength of the British Army in France. The valour, good shooting and determination shown by the troops in the line were of little avail against the vast superior numbers and although they defended till the last, the German forces were in possession of most of the forward zone by nightfall.*

*On the* ***22nd****, as the fog cleared, it became a day of great aerial activity with the Royal Flying corps carrying out low level attacks to relieve the pressure on the infantry. The advance of the German Army continued and fresh ground was taken.*

*On the* ***23rd*** *the line of the Crozat was taken and at noon the British headquarters ordered a new line to be prepared from*

*Peronnes to Arras, and at 5 pm the line on the Somme was ordered to be held at all costs. The German advance in the north had not made the advance anticipated and Hindenburg's plan was revised The new line of advance was to be in 3 sectors working north-west, west and south-west in an endeavour to separate the British and French armies.*
*On the* ***24th*** *more ground was lost, including the line of the Somme to within 3 miles of Peronnes . Philippe Petain's strategy was now to cover Paris, which would leave the British flank open. In desperation Sir Douglas Haig handed over his army south of the Somme to the French Commander General Fayolle.*
*The* ***25th*** *saw another day of intense air activity – the RFC being ordered "to bomb and shoot everything on the other side of the line. Very low flying is essential and all risks must be taken." The advance did not come up to expectations and the German High Command were most disappointed at their failure to force the 3rd Army withdrawal north and south of Arras.*
*The offensive continued through the* ***26th*** *and* ***27th March*** *but the only real gain was the taking of Montdidier from the French. It was obvious that the German advance was slowing down and later Crown Prince Rupert recorded that this day was "The turning point of the great offensive" The operation "Mars" was to begin against Arras by German troops who had been in preparation since the 25th . The attack followed the pattern of the 21st but even more gas shells were dropped on the artillery. Following the artillery bombardment the Germans advanced with 29 Divisions (13 in the front line) against the 8 divisions (6 in the front line) of the British. The principal effort was on a 3 mile front, just north of Scarpe. Small gains were made but by the late afternoon the attack had failed and by nightfall was formally halted. Only local attempts were to be made to hold the British. Even this was not a complete success.*

*The offensive slackened and stopped on the* ***29th . 4th and 5th April****, the last effort was carried out in an attempt to reach Amiens but against the British 3rd Army it was a complete failure. The official German report concludes: "The enemy resistance was beyond our powers."*

***Narrative of operations 28th March.*** *(Arras)*

*3.00am to 7.20am very heavy bombardment on trenches of the Brigade on the right. The sector held by the Battalion was also subjected to intermittent shelling*

*At 7.20 am the enemy endeavoured to advance from Johnson Lane, but were twice driven back by Rifle and L.G. fire from the trench held by B Company.*

*About 8.30 am the Brigade on my right started to withdraw from Jerusalem and Invergordon trenches and also from the trenches south of Cambrai road. At this time my front was still intact.*

*About 9.30 am the Battalion on my immediate right started to withdraw. The O.C. Of this Battalion informed me that his right was in the air. As I was still holding Lancer, I asked him to reoccupy Invergordon and form a flank to the Feuchy chapel crossroads. In the meantime I withdrew the Company of the Duke of Wellington's to form a defensive flank along the Pelves Lane from Lance avenue. This was successfully carried out. As every flank became more exposed, I ordered my right flank along the sunken road from Lancer Ave. (about H.29 B 5.7) to junction of Sunken road and Pelves Lane. The Duke's side slipping, so as to produce the flank to Invergordon. I ordered Lieut. Edmonde to collect what men he could and endeavour to establish himself in Invergordon at about H.28 d 8.0. This I believe he would have accomplished had not our own heavies shelled him out of it.*

*As troops on my right were still retiring and the enemy was west of the Feuchy Chapel crossroads and also hold Jerusalem and Grange Hill, I decided it was impossible to hold onto Lancer and protect the right flank. By this time B Company from Italian trench had been used to strengthen the right flank. The three Companies in Lancer received orders from me to fall back towards the army line – 1 Company being left as rear-guard to delay the enemy. I could see no British troops on my right. In fact the enemy was then in the Valley west of Feuchy Road, so I continued my withdrawal to Army Line.*
*a. I received orders from the 10th Infantry Brigade that no withdrawal was to take place. These instructions were issued to all company's. In my opinion the situation was such that a withdrawal was imperative to save the Battalion from being completely cut off .*
*b. I sent two messages to the Brigade stating the situation saying my position is becoming critical. About 2 pm I sent a message saying I was withdrawing to Army line.*
*Signed G.H.V. Lacom.*
*Lieut. Colonel,*
*Commanding 1st R.W.R.*

**March 29th** Fritz is still shelling very heavily but his infantry attack has been stopped.
We managed to push forward in the night and regained part of our lost ground.
We didn't know how the chaps have managed to do it, but we have full rations brought up.
We are all very tired but full of thanks and admiration for our Colonel.
A lot of shells into Arras.

**March 30th** The shelling is still terrific but their infantry have not made another big attack yet.
There have been a few patrol battles.
We are told that that all civilians have fled Arras.
They had been advised to leave over a month ago, so we are not surprised.
Our Casualties have been light considering the heavy fighting.
About sixty all told.
Weather has been good.

**March 31st** We made an attack at 4.00am this morning to regain a couple of trenches, to straighten out our line.
Had a rough time as they were strongly held but we managed to take them after about an hour's fighting.
We had about sixteen casualties, including two officers.
The German aeroplanes have been busy all day flying low to try to locate our new positions and estimate our strength.
Their guns have been shelling most of the trenches, but we are holding our ground.

**1918 April**

**April 1st** A fine bright day, but it is hard to believe that it is Easter.
We are under heavy shellfire most of the morning and I had a very lucky escape about midday. A shell burst very near to me.
When I had sorted myself out, I had only a scratch on my right hand, besides being shaken up.
Two pieces of shrapnel had also ripped my trousers.
I think that I went to Heaven and Hell in those few seconds.
The German aircraft have been flying low, giving their artillery the range. So you can guess it has been pretty hot.
It's been raining and things are a bit uncomfortable.

We are due to be relieved tonight.

**April 2nd** We were relieved just after midnight but only moved back six hundred yards, into a support trench.
We shall really be glad to get out for a few days, if only for a chance to get cleaned up and have a good wash.
We are still being shelled heavily but there has been no further infantry attack.
Getting some rain, so things are bit uncomfortable.

**April 3rd** Raining heavily all night and most of the day.
We are still under shellfire and getting a few casualties.
This last week casualties from shellfire are in the region of a hundred.
Shall be glad when we get relieved for a few days.
I think most of us are done in.

**April 4th** Still raining.
Had a three hour bombardment this morning.
We all think that Fritz is getting ready to have another go at us.
Shall be glad to get a rest.
It must be twenty days now since I had my boots off, so I reckon my feet must smell a bit fresh.

**April 5th** Relieved from the first line and moved back into the second line, near Blangy.
It was a very dark, wet night and we were wandering around for ages, trying to find our new position.
We found the line after about two hours.

**April 6th** We have been searching the area all day, trying to find a dugout to sleep in tonight.
Found one by 6pm, made it a bit more shipshape.

At 9 pm, eight of us got down to try to get some sleep.
We couldn't get to sleep and then realised that there was a peculiar smell in the dugout.

**April 7th** Just after midnight a couple of the chaps got up and fell flat on their faces.
We knew what the smell was – it is a gas that miners meet at times when they are digging underground.
Got out into the air all right but my head was spinning round.
Later in the night we had another sort of gas.
Fritz started again with his shells.
Six of the chaps including Captain McKenzie were gassed but we won't know until later how seriously.
Managed to find another dugout, for tonight.
Our Colonel has been sent home and he is to be relieved by Colonel Marriot.
Got down in the dugout at 9pm.

**April 8th** Had a good night's sleep and feel much better today.
It has been raining quite hard.
We were relieved by the 16th Canadians at about 9pm.
Marched to Blangy locks, where we met some motor lorries.
They took us about five miles, the other side of Arras, to an aerodrome on the St. Pol road.
There we slept in an aeroplane shed, but it was very cold and the ground wet.
Managed to wash my feet at long last

**April 9th** Fritz started to shell the camp this morning.
One of the cook houses was hit, luckily no-one was in it.
We had to move out of the sheds while the shelling was going on.

***<u>Official narrative : April 9th 1918</u>*** *saw an offensive similar to the pattern of the 21st March by 14 German divisions (8 in the front line ) against the position held by 3 Portuguese brigades. Within two hours the Portuguese were completely overwhelmed. Reserves were rushed in and the Germans halted at the limit of penetration, some 3½ miles. The following day a similar attack was launched and Armentieres evacuated as it was now under attack from the north and south and in danger of being cut off. The attack resumed on the 11th but with the exception of a thrust to within 5 miles of Hazebrouck very little ground was gained. The general position gave the British cause for much concern and resulted in the following message being attached to Sir Douglas Haig's order of the day - "There is no other course open to us but to fight it out. Every position must be held to the last man. There must be no retirement. With our backs to the wall and believing in justice of our cause each one must fight to the end. The safety of our homes and the freedom of mankind alike depend on the conduct of each one of us at this critical moment.*

**April 10th** Struck camp just before daybreak and scattered. We are due to return and encamp after dark.
If Fritz spots the camp he will most certainly start to shell, again. What a rest this has turned out to be.

**April 11th** Moved into some huts just outside Agnez-les-Duisans. The weather has improved.
Fed up with moving about.
We shall be glad to settle down and get a few days' rest.

**April 12th** All night we were under orders to move at a minutes notice.

At 12noon, moved off in motor lorries to Lillers near to La Bassee. Here the enemy have broken through the Portuguese held position.
Marched nearly all night to take up an outpost position.
We are attempting to find out exactly where the enemy has reached.
It was very sad to see the poor civilians flocking back through Lillers, carrying bundles of all their possessions.

**April 13th** We stayed the night in an empty outpost position and this morning we have pushed on to Hinges.
Met a Hun patrol near the canal. Captured the officer and three men.
We are amazed by the state of the villages.
The villagers have fled and left everything behind.
We took over the houses and used them for billets.

**April 14th** After a night in a house, we killed some fowl and rabbits and had a good feed.
A shell burst among us while we were drawing rations, killing Lance Corporal Bishop and wounding three others.
I was knocked down by the force of the explosion and got covered in dirt.
It has shaken me up badly, but have only bruises, so my luck holds.
I'm very tired though.

**April 15th** Orders to prepare to attack at 5.30pm.
The enemy is massing troops, in the Picault wood across the canal in front of us.
We are to attempt a break through and split them up.
Our artillery opened a bombardment at 5.15pm but some of the shells fell short.

We had casualties among our own men.
There was also damage to the pontoon bridge, over which we were to advance.
An officer called on six of us to go with him, to repair the pontoon.
Had a hell of a time with enemy shells, dropping close by in the water and on the banks.
Our attack started half an hour late at 6pm and we advanced on the wood which was still alive with machine guns.
The enemy put up a strong resistance, but we managed to gain four hundred yards, capturing eight machine guns and taking some prisoners but at a terrible cost.
We have lost nearly four hundred of the men, which is just about half.
Our prisoners have been questioned and we found out they were about to advance in three waves with their cavalry in support.

**April 16th** We spent most of a very cold night digging and bringing up rations and now we all feel absolutely worn out.
Managed to hold the position without much difficulty.

***Official narrative April 1918:***
*The 12th to 16th April saw the offensive diminishing although the heavy fighting for local vantage points took place all along the front, the only German success being at Bailleul. The offensive was renewed with vigour on the 17th but was a complete failure and it collapsed after 2 hours. The French south of the Somme carried out a counter offensive and were successful in coming into line with the British troops further north. The German offensive continued with heavy fighting but limited success until the 30th April when the German chiefs of Staff ordered the offensive to be suspended. The total*

*casualties for the period 21st of March to 30th April killed and wounded : German 348,000*
*British 239.793,*
*French 92,004*

**April 17th** The Seaforths have taken over our position on the line.
We have moved over to the right, to form a link from the Seaforths to the 61st Division.
Came under a heavy artillery bombardment as we reached this position and had twenty nine casualties.
The weather is keeping bitter cold.

**April 18th** Fritz opened a heavy bombardment at 1.00am on the Seaforths and ourselves, which lasted until 5.30am.
As the barrage lifted, the Hun mounted an infantry attack on our left.
A party of them got a pontoon bridge partially across the canal but the Seaforths surrounded them, taking one hundred and twenty prisoners.
Their other attacks were repulsed at all points.
We are told we shall be relieved tonight.
Relieved at 9.30pm and went a short distance back in reserve.
Got shelled on the way out, but no casualties.

**April 19th** Stopped in the top storey of an old château but Fritz started to shell it, so we had to move out.
Our new doctor is an American and he has gone sick because of the shelling.
He has only been with us five days.
Orders to move up in reserve at 5.30pm.

**April 20th** We are in support, in Gonnehem village, close to the first line.
Nearly all the civilians have left everything behind, except their money and valuables.
Poor devils, it's very hard for them.
While the shelling was quiet, one or two of them came back last night to fetch a few more of their things.
Our lines of communication were cut this morning, so we had to give them just twenty minutes to get out.
Killed some fowl today and had a real good feed, which helped to buck us up a bit.
This afternoon we became real farmer's boys.
I fed a cow to keep it quiet, while Ingram was milking it.
Had one or two minor disasters but managed to get a bucket and a half of milk.
Weather very good.
We have only had our boots off three nights this month.

**April 21st** After having snow and hail, the last three days have been grand.
Bar the shelling, things are fairly quiet today.
The government officials rounded up all the cattle but we managed to find a cow and a calf that they missed.
At midnight when things were quiet, Golby killed the calf and we all helped to dress it.
We are sure to be shot if we get caught, but we managed everything all right and we have buried the skin and the offal without being seen.

**April 22nd** We went on the scout and got a couple of fowl and plenty of potatoes for dinner.
Had a bit of fun with the cow. I was feeding her while Porky was trying to milk her.

Apart from the cow getting her foot in the bucket once or twice we managed nearly two full buckets.

**April 23rd** Fritz keeps shelling pretty heavily, but the farm still holds on.
We had a sudden order to move up in support at 10.30pm, so we had to leave the poor old cow.
We got to our new position about midnight.

**April 24th** We have been busy digging trenches.
At present we are stopping in an old barn but we expect Fritz will blow it up any time.
He has been shelling very heavily all night but he has not made any attack.

**April 25th** Another night of trench digging.
Aeroplanes have been busy trying to find our positions.
At 5pm Fritz started to bombard us with heavy artillery.
We had to move out of the barn, into a dugout that we have been making a bit further on, over to our left.
It's a good thing we did, Fritz dropped a high explosive shell onto the barn and knocked it flat.

**April 26th** Digging again.
We have been busy making a new dugout and trench for the Headquarters staff.
Our new Colonel is a real dugout man.
As soon as the shelling gets a bit hot, down he goes.
Darky and Beresford went to Robecq today.
All the civilians have been shelled out. They came back with a pile of boots, but they found out they were all odd sizes.

**April 27th** Heavy bombardment in the night and our ration transport was smashed up with shellfire.
Four were killed, five wounded and five horses killed.
A very misty day so we were out digging trenches in the mist.

**April 28th** Shelling again in the night but quieter in the day time.
At 9pm, we moved further over to the left, to a barn, just behind the lines.
I believe this place is shelled regularly.

**April 29th** Digging again to make this place more shell proof.
It's dig, dig, dig all day and night.
No sooner do we get a place dug out and sandbagged, then we are on the move again.
Just realised it is now three weeks since I had my boots off.

**Apri1 30th** We are still digging away and trying to make this place shell proof.
We have been banking the cellar up, so it will be safe when Fritz starts shelling.
He shells us every night, but he has not hit this farm yet.
Weather very dull and cloudy.

**1918 May**

**May 1st** The Colonel's cellar was finished about 8.30pm. Most of the chaps are feeling quite queer so they sent a medical orderly down to take temperatures.
Eight have been sent to the hospital.
I think that it is some kind of fever.
The doctor doesn't seem to know what it is.

**May 2nd** The shelling on both sides is very heavy.
We were relieved at 11pm by the Somerset, then went back into reserve in the village of Busnettes.

**May 3rd** Arrived at the village about 2am.
All absolutely worn out and wet.
Had some food and a tot of rum and went to sleep.

**May 4th** We are told that we are here for a four day rest.
Spent the day having a good wash down, cleaning uniforms and kit.
Raining heavily.

**May 5th** Still raining.
This is a very flat country here and the water doesn't drain away. The old enemy, mud with us again.

**May 6th** Started for the trenches at 7pm.
We had to go cross country because Fritz is shelling the roads again.
Plodded our way across wet and muddy fields.
Reached the firing line, without trouble, by midnight.
The front line here consists mainly of shell holes and there is very little cover.

**May 7th** Fairly quiet night and then a misty day.
Bosch aeroplanes have been flying very low in the mist, trying to locate our positions.
We came under heavy shelling at 9pm and a heavy bombardment at 10.30pm.

**May 8th** The shelling has been going on and off all night but we have been lucky and only had two casualties.

The day turned out fine and the aeroplanes on both sides have been busy all day.
We came under heavy shell fire at 8.30pm, until 2am.
They concentrated most of it on our batteries, using gas shells.
The Headquarters staff expected an attack so we had to stand to in readiness all night.

**May 9th** Stood to all night and have been busy making the positions stronger.
Fritz bombarded us with gas shells from 3am to 5am.
The wind changed and drifted it from us, to our artillery.
One or two of the gunners were gassed.
Our artillery gave them a terrific bombardment between 10pm and 11pm.

**May 10th** Fairly quiet night, on guard duty until 3am.
Fritz then started to retaliate, with gas shells.
One hit the first aid post.
All four doctors and the orderlies suffered from the effect of gas.

**May 11th** We are having a really rough time here with shelling, we are losing four or five men every day.
The enemy gassed us again today.
Luckily only one or two felt the effects.
Lieutenant Streeton and Tanby Gibson were killed early this morning.
Two of the very best.

**May 12th** The enemy fairly quiet in the night and early in the day.
At 10.30pm they sent over a barrage of sneezing and gas shells but we were very quick to act and only the dog was affected.

We are all feeling the strain of the last few days but we are managing to get full rations up.
Shall be glad to be relieved.

**May 13th** Raining and miserable day, not much shelter here.
The enemy is still quiet.

**May 14th** Heavy rain in the night and our artillery have been very busy.
Our artillery put up a heavy barrage on the enemy lines, every half hour between 10 pm and 2am.
Intelligence thought that the enemy front line was being relieved.

**May 15th** Did a small raid in the night and captured two prisoners, belonging to the 8th Jacques Rifles.
They had orders to hold their positions at all cost.
A hot sunny day with lots of aeroplanes and observation balloons up.
We dare not move in daylight for fear of giving away our position. Relieved at 10pm, by the Rifle Brigade.
During these last nine days in the front line, we have had more than fifty casualties.

**May 16th** Moved back in reserve at Busnettes for a four day rest.
Had a good sleep and clean-up.
The weather is grand.

**May 17th** Enemy bombers over in the night.
No real damage done and no casualties.
Had a drill parade and military training.
What a rest!

**May 18th** Weather remains good.
Routine training and drill.

**May 19th** Marched up to the trenches, got there without any trouble about 10.30pm.
Plenty of wind at night but no attacks.

**May 20th** Enemy fairly quiet and we are all expecting an attack but so far nothing has happened.

**May 21st** Fairly quiet night but off we go digging yet another dugout for the Colonel.

**May 22nd** The digging goes on.
We work from 9am to 2am, the following morning, in shifts.
We then go on gas sentry duty. The enemy has started shelling again but so far no sign of an attack.

**May 23rd** Heavy rain in the night and the day spent digging.
The enemy have sent over gas shells but no casualties.

**May 24th** Rain again in the night and now this place is like a swamp.
We are all fed up with this dugout digging and are getting short of water.

**May 25th** The day dawned fine but dull.
Fritz has been shelling heavy this last couple of days, but he has not attacked.
During the shelling today there were plenty of splinters flying about but no casualties.

Four men in C. Company got gassed, when they drank some water from a shell hole.

**May 26th** We have at last finished the dugout and the enemy has been fairly quiet.
A fairly restful day.
Full rations.

**May 27th** Heavy shelling.
They managed to smash our Brigade headquarters but only two men wounded and two pet dogs killed.
We were relieved at 11pm and got out without any trouble.

**1918 June**

**May 28th to June 1st** Arrived at Busnettes in reserve, during the night and spent the first day having a good clean-up.
Regular "rest" routine of parades and training.
Fritz has been coming over, shelling the village every night.
We have had a couple of bombing raids by aeroplanes, on the clear nights.
We had one killed and six wounded.

**June 2nd** Marched to the firing line between Gonnehem and Robecq and arrived at 10.30pm.
At 11pm, Fritz bombarded us with sneezing gas shells and continued on and off until 3am.
It left me with sore and bloodshot eyes and a rotten headache.

**June 3rd** Enemy artillery fairly active night and day but the weather is splendid and the rations fairly good.

**June 4th** Weather still very good and the artillery active.
Darky Burgess dug up a pretty metal vase. He kidded a fellow that it was silver. The fellow gave him twenty francs for it.

**June 5th** Still under gas shell bombardment.
Further up the line, at Hinges just north of Bethune, the Black Watch have been shelled with a new gas.
If you get a good dose, it makes you temporarily blind.

**June 6th** Our artillery had a really good go at the enemy in the night.
They retaliated with gas shells on our support company, who were expecting it and got their masks on smartly.

**June 7th** Fairly quiet night and day.
Plenty of aeroplanes about but very little enemy action.
After dark, we went out on patrol to try and bring a prisoner back for information.
Up to now we have not succeeded.
A fine bright day.

**June 8th** Artillery fairly active on a lovely fine day.
At 10.30pm Fritz raided our left sector but was driven back.
We are fully expecting him to launch a full scale attack here, in the near future.
Rations good lately.

**June 9th** Both sides have been bombarding heavily and we had some rain.
Scotty has been making jam tarts with soaked biscuits but they are terrible.

**June 10th** In the night we were bombarded with gas shells again but no casualties.
Some fellows were sent to hospital feeling queer.
The doctor said it was caused by eating potatoes, out of ground which had been gassed.

**June 11th** Enemy very active.
The "Jocks" made a bombing raid in the night but it was a failure. Fritz caught a B. Company patrol in an ambush, three killed, three wounded and one missing- believed captured.

**June 12th** A lovely day and we are still getting good rations.
Artillery fire on both sides very active.

**June 13th** Two companies went back into reserve.
We have to stop with any company in the line.
We are to help to reinforce the 3rd Division to carry out an advance, to straighten the line.

**June 14th** Went into action with the 3rd Division and it was a great success.
We took one hundred and eighty nine prisoners and a few machine guns.
Our casualties only about fifty.
The prisoners belong to the regiment which first entered Belgium in 1914.

**June 15th** Marched back to join our other two Companies, in reserve.
Had a good clean up.

**June 16th** During the night we were out on working parties, building up the front line system.

In the afternoon we had a lecture from the Colonel, telling us that the General officer Commanding wished to congratulate those who had worked with the 3rd Division in the attack.
Our Colonel said he was concerned with the rate of crime in the Brigade.
I must say there has been more crime since he came, than we had in the last two years.

**June 17th and 18th** Working party duties up the line at night.
For once, a good rest during the day.
Rations still good.
Orders to go back to the firing line tomorrow.

**June 19th** We marched through a storm to the firing line but near Robecq had to wait for the shelling to ease off before we attempted to relieve.
At midnight things went quiet so we went in without any casualty.

**June 20th** Another of the old boys was killed this morning.
The weather is very rough.
Its blowing hard and raining nearly all night.
Enemy fairly quiet.

**June 21st** The weather is still rough.
The rations are good and the enemy very quiet.

**June 22nd** Enemy quiet again but a very cold wind is blowing and we have had some rain.

**June 23rd** Enemy still quiet.
Almost too quiet for our peace of mind.
They must be getting ready for something.

**June 24th** We have got a kind of fever knocking around.
The chaps just have no strength at all.
Five or six, every day, have been taken back to the hospital.
At about midnight the 61st Division on our right made a bombing raid.
Fritz really opened up with his shells.
I expect he thought that it was the start of a full attack.
More of the chaps sent back to hospital with this new illness.

**June 25th** Very cold for this time of the year, more like October than June, at night.
The enemy have been very quiet again.

**June 26th** More of the chaps taken ill and the doctors told us that it was caused by bites from a type of bug which injects poison into the blood stream.
Password for today : " Have you seen the bug?"

**June 27th and 28th** We are livening things up a bit here.
The division on our right have taken Merville and about five hundred prisoners, today.
The air is alive with enemy bombing planes every night that it is fine.
It almost makes you wish for dirty weather.

**June 29th** A bright night and lots of enemy bombing aircraft about.
A quiet day.
In a break from the shelling we were able to go out and dig up some new potatoes at Robecq.

**June 30th** A fairly quiet day which was followed by a misty day. At 9.30am we carried out a surprise bombing raid in the mist, assisted by a smoke screen, on our right flank. We went over as soon as the artillery opened fire.

We caught them groggy, as most of them were having a nap. We killed fifty and brought back nine prisoners, three of them were wearing the Iron Cross.

We only lost one killed, one missing and eight wounded.

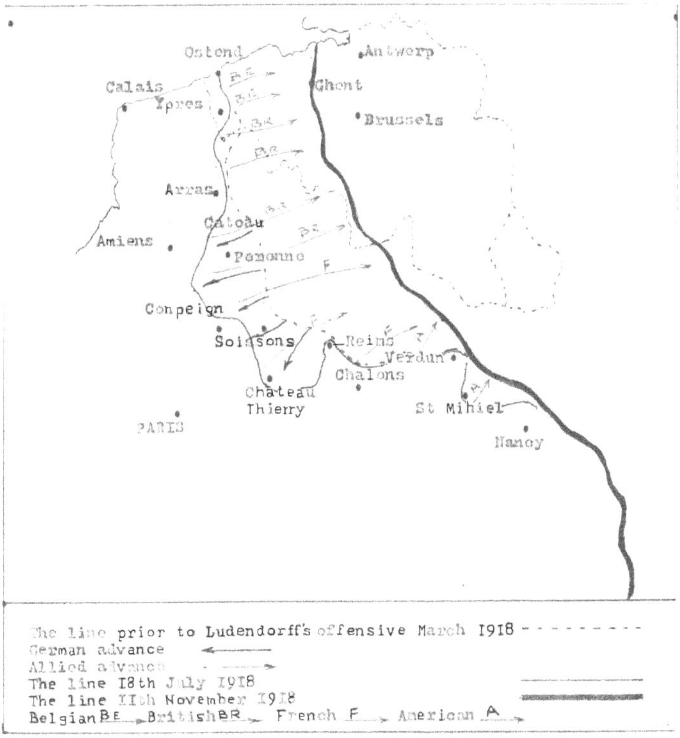


**Map 5. July 1918**

Ludendorff's Offensive July 1918, Arras

**1918 July**

**July 1st** Fritz has been shelling heavily again, since our raid.
A lovely warm day, sunny and dry.
Plenty of aeroplanes about.
Were relieved at 11pm and got out without any casualties.
We go in reserve to Busnettes, for six days.

**July 2nd** Had a good sleep despite Fritz dropping bombs in the area, which he seems to do every fine night.
A good clean up and then the old routine of drill parades and training.
Rations good.

**July 3rd** Went out in the night on the scout and managed to find some new potatoes and peas in one of the gardens.
We had a grand dinner.

**July 4th** Went out again, at night, for more potatoes and peas but found to our surprise that the house was inhabited.
The chap was sitting waiting for us.
We outflanked him and got back without being spotted.

**July 5th and 6th** Routine of parades and training.
However, we were allowed out during the afternoon to go into the village.

**July 7th** We hear that Fritz has carried out a raid on the trench that we are due to take over from the King's Own.
They have taken a prisoner.
We had a rough time getting to the firing line – the roads being shelled and bombed, on and off all night. They must have got

information from the prisoner and knew that we were coming to relieve.
It was a rough passage but we managed to get in without loss.

**July 8th** Artillery on both sides very active.
The weather is very warm and muggy and the whole place is alive with mosquitoes and horse flies.
We have nearly all been stung at least once a day.
The horse fly stings are quite unpleasant.
It makes you wish for the cold weather.

**July 9th** A fairly quiet, warm night. Fritz started off with his gas shells this morning.
Having very heavy rainstorms.
We have a lot of rats here, so our dogs have been busy.
The puppy managed to catch one. The rat hung onto the puppy's nose and frightened him nearly to death.

**July 10th** Enemy artillery active again.
Fritz smashed up one of machine gun posts in the doorway of the farmhouse, killing the officer and wounding four others.
They have given us a substitute for milk, it looks like white sand. Scotty put some in the tea.
It made the top of the tea as greasy as soup and the rest of the stuff settled at the bottom.
It didn't even change the colour of the tea.
I'd sooner have jam in my tea.

**Lewis machine gun post at Farm house.**
(Vickers before 1916.)

**July 11th** Artillery have been very active on both sides.
Two of our Company were killed by shellfire.
The rain is making things rather rough.
We are able to get some field peas and potatoes, every now and then.

**July 12th** Spent the night with a digging party making a new dugout for our first aid post.
We need to give a bit more protection for the wounded and sick.

**July 13th** Fairly quiet night and a dry day.
Our aeroplanes have been out, flying low, machine gunning the enemy lines.
One of them force-landed just behind the line, with engine trouble.

The mechanics came up and worked on it at nightfall. We levelled the ground a bit and it got off in the dark.

**July 14th** Just a shower or two today.
Tug Wilson's puppy had another go at rat catching.
This time the rat just jumped on him and nearly frightened him to death.
Heavy shelling by Fritz at 10.30pm, but luckily no casualties.

**July 15th** A showery day.
There is a terrific bombardment going on to our far right, so we all expect that Fritz has started his offensive in that sector.
We don't know if it will extend to us, but we are all ready for it.
He has been shelling really heavily lately.

**July 16th** There is a really big battle raging on our right, but we can't get any news of it.
Plenty of aeroplanes bombing the area all night.
"Big Dinner", our corporal, has had a tin of milk in his haversack for at least a fortnight.
Scotty managed to get it and swapped it for an empty one.

**July 17th** Heavy artillery duels, particularly on our far right, but no news has come through about the offensive by Fritz.

**July 18th** Some artillery activity during the night, from both sides.
The Duke of Wellingtons made a raid with two hundred men at 2.30pm.
They captured about thirty prisoners.
The Dukes had two killed and eleven wounded.
Fritz then shelled our trenches very heavily.
The Seaforths had about seven casualties.

We had two killed and five wounded.
A mortar trench blew up, killing six of the team.

**July 19th** Still under heavy shellfire.
Fritz must have brought more guns up, as he gave us a heavy night.
One of his 5.9's dropped on one of our Lewis gun teams, which killed four and wounded six.
Our artillery retaliated and laid barrage after barrage on his lines, in the pouring rain.

**July 20th** Quiet today, but "Big Dinner" discovered his milk loss. He suspects Scotty but he can't prove anything and he is making a real fuss about it.

**July 21st** Shelling again night and day but much lighter guns.
Relieved from the front line at 11.30pm and went back in reserve to Busnettes.
This place gets shelled and bombed at night.

**July 22nd** In billets at a house in the village.
Had a good clean up and then the usual parade and training.

**July 23rd** A draft of one hundred and seventy five men joined us today, most of them from home.
We have been busy training so I expect that something big is coming, soon.

**July 24th** Enemy bombers again active in the area, during the night.
Usual routine of training during the day.
The weather has been rough and wet.

**July 25th** Fritz started shelling this village at 1.40am.
We were very lucky as they hit the house facing us, killing three of B. Company and wounding five.
They moved us away to another house, near a dangerous crossroad.
Had a sporting event in the afternoon, but it was a very tame affair compared with last year.
The Follies gave us a real good show in the evening.
So had a real good day.

**July 26th** Fritz shelled the village again, last night but no casualties.
The weather is still showery and windy.
Orders to move up to the line tomorrow.

**July 27th** Marched up to the front line trenches and got there at about 10 pm.
A section of D. Company were crossing the canal on the barrel bridge, when it turned turtle and pitched about ten of them into the water.
Lance Corporal Moore, whom I knew before I transferred to Headquarters Company, got wedged between the bridge and the bottom of the canal.
They couldn't find him until daylight.

**July 28th** A nice fine day. We went to Robecq scouting for potatoes but we only found about six pounds, before Fritz started shelling the village.
We had to get out quickly.
Have been under heavy shellfire in the trenches all day but only two killed.

One of the Somersets picked up a German egg bomb to heave it back but it went off in his hand and he died of his wounds later.

**July 29th** The artillery is still active.
We had a two franc bet with a chap called Marks, a proper yokel from somewhere Worcester way. He was challenged to eat five small and two large tins of jam for his tea.
He nearly burst and had to give up on the 5th . It was worth our jam ration to get so much fun out of it.

**July 30th** Stormy and wet and the artillery active at night.
Went for a scout for potatoes and found some horse beans. We boiled them for a fair time and they were quite tasty, much like broad beans.

**July 31st** Still raining and windy.
Some of the chaps went on patrol in the night to find the enemy forward post.
They came back empty handed.

**1918 August**

**August 1st** Enemy still active at night but quieter during the day.
Artillery on both sides have been very active, every night.
The expected offensive has not happened so we will just have to wait and see.

**August 2nd** Started to make some deep dugouts for the winter. It's low lying country here and will be very wet if we get the heavy rain and snow later.

One of our fighting patrols captured a German trench mortar gun this morning.
Unfortunately the enemy got clear.

**August 3rd** Fritz has been shelling the billet, of the reserve troops, at L'Ecleme.
The Seaforths had eight killed and eight wounded.
Weather still rough and plenty of water about.

**August 4th** Heavy rain in the night and a stormy day. If this keeps up we shall be flooded out.
Had an issue of frozen rabbits today, instead of bully beef.
With our horse beans they made a good meal.
Another issue of powdered milk, I think it is ground coconut, terrible stuff.

**August 5th** Our Colonel has been taken to hospital.
Fritz has retired a little to our right.
Intelligence think he may be preparing to move back at our position.
We have to send patrols out night and day to keep in touch with our intelligence.

**August 6th** Heavy shelling during the night.
The enemy aircraft have been bombing our reserve lines and rest camps.
Orders to be ready to start an offensive, at a moment's notice.

**August 7th** The Germans have started their retreat.
Our patrols were in touch at daybreak and had some very difficult fighting.
Fritz has left behind snipers and machine gun posts, to fight a rear-guard action in the heart of the wood.

The wood was so thick in parts, that we were right up to the snipers before we located them.
In some cases, they opened up at us only a matter of yards away. It was just luck who they aimed at and who they didn't.
Made good use of the cover of tree trunks and our Regiment gained about a thousand yards.
We have been following up and driving the enemy rear-guard back as fast as we can, but it is very dangerous fighting.
Their machine gun positions are so hard to locate.
All sorts of booby traps are set against the advancing troops.
We have lost about twenty men today, including the Officer in charge of C. Company.
He was a really fine officer and gentleman.

**August 8th** We are meeting very heavy resistance.
Have lost track of Mr Horsley and twelve men of C. Company.
I expect that they fell into an ambush and got cut off.
Have managed to advance about another thousand yards.
We reckon this is very good going, without cavalry or tank support.
The weather has been fine and dry.

**August 9th to 22nd** The diaries for this period have at some time been soaking and are unreadable.

**August 23rd** Still following the retreating enemy, driving his rear-guard back.
Moving forward fast but it is very difficult fighting as their gun positions are so well hidden.

**August 24th and 25th** Relieved from the firing line and told that we are due for a long rest.
On the march for two days.

At the end of the second day, we stayed at Perns for the night.

**August 26th** Had sudden orders to move at once in battle order and had a twelve hour march to St. Eloie (Arras sector). We were all done in but had a good rest.

**August 27th** Had a good clean up.
In the evening went into the village and managed to buy some real vintage French wine.
It was really beautiful stuff.
Had a grand evening with a sing song and some good food.

**August 28th** Orders to move to the firing lines.
We came under heavy shellfire, about three miles short of our position.
Had about twelve casualties.
The limbers and horses on the Arras – Cambrai road have had a hell of a time of it.
The road was a shambles through the shelling.
We reached our position and relieved the 4th Canadian Division, just before midnight.

**August 29th** Advanced our position a little.
The enemy were bombing the trenches from the air during the night.
Artillery are very active night and day.
Orders to be in readiness, to advance, in the early morning.

**August 30th** At 5am we mounted an attack on the Hindenburg line.
Eventually reached it after meeting heavy resistance and suffering high casualties.
Our Battalion alone suffering thirty killed or wounded.

We reached our objective and are holding out.

**August 31st** At dawn the enemy launched a counter-attack all along this part of the line, which was held and then repulsed.
A Canadian Division joined us in the evening and are going with us at dawn tomorrow.

**1918 September**

**September 1st** The artillery opened their barrage at 5.00am and at 5.03am we went over. The first part of the action saw some bitter fighting with the enemy desperately trying to hold out but when the tanks got up with us his resistance faded and by 9.00am, we were well on the move forward. We have captured a great many prisoners today and they are all good fighting units, Prussian Guards, Jaquers, Saxons and Bavarians. From information received they were due to mount an attack at 5.10 am, so this would account for their state of readiness and their strength of fighting in the early stages of the battle.

**September 2nd** The great advance continues and today we are acting in support.
We were subject to heavy shelling, from our flank.
Our own artillery have done a wonderful job in, keeping up with us and giving us supporting cover.

**September 3rd** Moved back in reserve, to a captured enemy trench.
This was their front line near the Arras – Cambrai road.
The road is shelled with his heaviest guns.
Fritz also bombs by aircraft, day and night.
We go back for a rest in the morning.

One of the saddest sights I have seen in the battle : "One of our chaps had a shell burst very near to him. He was just groping about blind because blood was streaming from his nose, mouth and ears and he said he could not see".
We led him to the doctor, at the first aid post, who said that the concussion had burst his eardrums and his eyes.
Poor chap. He will be totally blind for the rest of his life.

**September 4th** Moved back to the village called Bailleul Aux Cornailles, which is about eight kilometres from St. Pol.
We are here for a rest.

**September 5th** We had a really good night's sleep and during the day paraded for the Colonel in Charge of the Canadian Division, to which we were attached for our last offensive.
He congratulated us on our efforts and on our splendid combined victory.
He said that he was proud to have had us under his command.

**September 6th** Went on escort to Coyecques, about thirty miles away, to fetch back a fellow from hospital.
He was there with self-inflicted wounds.
It took us three days to get there and back. Travelling was terribly slow.
On the first day we only managed to get to Aire, so we stayed there overnight.

**September 7th** Had a look round Aire before proceeding on to the hospital at Coyecques.
Fritz bombed this place quite heavily in the night, but the cathedral is only slightly damaged.
It's a splendid place inside, absolutely beautiful.

**Louvain, showing scale of damage.**

**September 8th** Went on to the hospital to collect our prisoner and decided that it would be best to stay there until early next morning.
We should then have a full day's travelling to return the prisoner, rather than be saddled with him overnight on the way.

**September 9th** Returned to Brigade Headquarters with the prisoner without incident.
I don't know whether he will be shot or get long term imprisonment

**September 10th** Had a good night's sleep and feel much better for it.
We were joined by two drafts, about two hundred men, to make us up to strength.
I expect we shall soon be at it again.

**September 11th to 15th** Five days of regular routine of quiet nights.
Drill parades and extensive military training during the day.
We are working with the new draft to get them up to scratch.
Our Divisional General Matheson has gone away and it is rumoured that he is in trouble, for not making sure that we had our entitlement of rest periods during the last four months.
This is one of his responsibilities.

**September 16th** They have taken my home address, for leave, but I expect that it will be a month or two before it comes to my turn.
Two of our chaps have gone to Paris, on a nine days leave.
I expect they will have a really good time but I cannot afford to do it.
**September 17th** Our dear Sergeant cook gave us a birthday yesterday.
He said he had managed to get some vegetables for us.
He brought one cabbage and four carrots for thirty seven men.
I wonder if he was trying to overfeed us all! He has a real sense of humour.

**September 18th** Sudden orders to proceed to the trenches.
We marched at 12.30 to Tincques.
Got into motor buses to be driven to greater subway near to Monchy, which is about five miles east of Arras.
Marched to the trenches.
We are holding the line to the right of Eglaine, in front of Dury.
Fritz has dammed the River Scarpe that runs between us.
There is a clear sheet of water nearly a mile in width, in front of us.
If we send any patrols over, they have got to go over on a raft.
He has done this to hold up our advance.

**September 19th to 24th** We are holding the position until the water borne tactics are sorted out.
Some of the engineers' experts have been here to see if they can stop the water from flooding.
So far they have had no luck.
We have been getting things ready for another advance.
I believe it starts on the 25th, if Fritz doesn't retire from our front.
We have got to get over the water on rafts.
We look like having a really rough job.
If our flanks advance they will force the enemy out of their present position.
The enemy gassed us this afternoon but I only got what they call "a bite".
Just enough to let you know that there is a war on.

**September 25th** We were moved back, in reserve, during the night about half a mile from the position we were holding.
We got out without casualties.
Fritz has been busy again with his gas shells.
They make your chest sore if you get a mouthful.

**September 26th** The enemy is shelling this area with very heavy guns from miles away.
It's getting very cold in the night now.
Only have our rum ration about one night in three, so on the other nights we feel that we really need it.

***The Second battle of Arras. The Battle of the Scarpe.***

*The allied operations of the 30th August, continuing to the 3rd September were a great success. The only sector not in advance was on the Somme north of Peronnes where the flooded state of the ground was considered too difficult. During the night of the 2nd and 3rd September, after heavy fighting, the Germans withdrew to the Hindenburg position at its maximum – this amounted to some 13 miles near St. Quentin. By the night of 3rd and 4th September the entire salient won by the Germans in March had been abandoned and some consolidation of the line had taken place by the allied troops. The 4th September a day of rest and preparation for the 3rd and 4th Armies.*

*The advance continued on the Somme for some 5 more days and the new positions fortified. On the 12th September the Americans mounted their attack on the Saint Mihiel sector between the Moselle and the Meuse supported by the French and British aircraft and French tanks. The attack was launched in thick fog and within 36 hours the objective had been reached depriving the German Army of the last of its four salients. Between 12th and 26th September the allied advances continued and fierce battles were fought by the 3rd Army on the 12th September. ( The Battle of Havrincourt ) and on the 18th by the 4th Army (The battle of Epehy).*

*The ground gained in the British Army offensive between the 8th August and 26th September was an average of 25 miles on a 40 mile front.*

**September 27th** The divisions, on our right, have been attacking.
We have heard that it was very successful.
They are moving towards Cambrai.
Now we wait until our left flank comes up before we will be able to do anything.

**September 28th** One of the Company patrols got in a boat to try and get across the water.
They were dodging about to avoid Fritz's machine gun fire when the boat overturned.
They all got back all right and were sent back to get their kit dry.

**September 29th** Weather has been rough this last week but the wind dries the mud up fairly well.
We expect Fritz to pick up again any day.
Plenty of patrols to do.

**September 30th** Weather is keeping rather rough.
We have been getting a rum issue but only one night in three.
It's cold enough to want it every night.
We are going back about half a mile in reserve for a few days.

**1918 October**
**October 1st** No entry made.

**October 2nd** Still under some shellfire but our artillery are very active.
They are sending over at least three shells to every one we receive, so I reckon old Fritz is having a rough time of it.

A six inch heavy gun, of our artillery was in action this morning.
Unfortunately one of its shells hit one of own aircraft.
A chance in a million.
The aircraft just burst to pieces and the poor chaps in it must have been killed instantly.
It's the first time that I have seen an aeroplane hit by our own artillery.

**October 3rd to 4th** No entry made.

**October 5th** The enemy has been fairly quiet, only bombing at night.
The weather has been very rough with plenty of rain.
I believe the Canadians will relieve us tomorrow.

**October 6th** Relieved by the 1st Canadian Division just after midnight and marched ten miles back to Arras.
We stayed the night in the museum, or what is left of it.

**October 7th** A free morning, so we went back to look round Arras.
Fritz has really knocked this place about, this last offensive.
A lot of the civilians have come back but all the estaminets are closed to the troops.
I bought an apple, they charged me four pence for it.
We left here at 3pm and marched some eleven kilometres, to Simecourt, for a few days' rest.
Had a good clean-up and sorted out our kit.

**October 8th to 10th** No entry made.

**October 11th** Sudden orders to move.
We marched for about two miles and then got in buses to Rollancourt.
From there marched to a village, about a mile from Cambrai.
All the villages are either smashed to pieces with shellfire or burned down.
Every bridge has been blown up in Cambrai and about half the town has been burned down.
It is as bad as Arras.

**October 12th** Started to advance in a north-easterly direction, almost as soon as we had settled in.
The enemy is really on the move.
Weather quite good.
Fairly warm for October with light rain.

**October 13th** We are scotching up the enemy, forcing him to continue to retire.
They are firing nearly every village and leaving a tremendous amount of booby traps and land mines.
The engineers are destroying them as fast as they can.
We have stopped at Naves, which is about five miles north-east from Cambrai.
The enemy is shelling this place, on and off, day and night.
We have great difficulty with our supply of water because the enemy has poisoned all the wells and reservoirs.

**October 14th to 17th** The weather is very bad, raining a lot.
Things have eased up for a few days.
Still at Naves.
Fritz has blown up as many bridges and railway lines as he could. The enemy had to move on before they could finish the work of destruction.

We are getting ready to start another big battle.

**October 18th** We marched to the forward position, to relieve "The Dukes" and had one of the worse shell bombardment of our lives. Went through shellfire for about two miles.
We never had such a rough time before, and the luck of it was we only had one wounded out of sixty.
Eventually, we stopped at Villers-De-Couche.
He gassed and shelled it all night.
"The Duke's" have had over forty men sent back to hospital, gassed.

**October 19th** Very heavy shelling of our position, all night and part of the day.
It is raining very hard.
Our artillery cannot shell the village in front of us, as it is reported that there is about a thousand civilians in it.

**October 20th** Raining very heavily and we are standing to from midnight to continue our offensive.
At 2am our artillery opened up firing over the village and we started our attack.
The only resistance that we encountered was from Fritz's long range guns and a few machine gunners.
The enemy are attempting a rapid retirement.
Today we have been meeting some of the civilians who are coming back, out of the firing area.
It makes your heart bleed for them.
They have been living down in cellars, afraid to move.
As Fritz left he shelled it heavily, knowing they were there.
I could feel tears in my eyes for them.
The very old people are nearly broken hearted.

**October 21st** We advanced to the village of Saulzoir.
Most of the civilians have left in a hurry, leaving everything behind them.
We are told that the Germans sent some of the villagers out to the front of the village and then shot them.
I should not like to say if it was true, as a lot of them tell different tales.
Most of them cried with joy at being released.
We insisted that they leave the village, knowing the Huns habit of gas shelling at night.

**October 22nd** Very heavy enemy shelling during the night, so it was a good thing that we moved the civilians out.
It has been raining hard again for these last two days so there is plenty of mud about.
We are living well here on the food that the villagers left in their cellars.
They had been living in them before they were evacuated.

**October 23rd** Sudden orders to move at 5pm.
Eight of us took some small bridges, near the front line.
We then spent the night digging holes for the rest of the men, to use as a jumping off position for the attack.

**October 24th** We finished our digging at 3.30am, which was our time limit.
At 4.00am, our artillery opened a splendid barrage on the enemy front line.
They then started a creeping barrage, which moves forward, in front of the advancing infantry.
It was a magnificent attack.
The artillery laid barrage after barrage and we just followed it up for almost two miles capturing a large village, taking one

hundred and fifty prisoners, twelve machine guns and two trench mortars guns.
It went just as planned and our losses were only four men killed and ninety six wounded.
At nightfall we were relieved by the King's Own, who are due to continue the advance in the morning.

**October 25th** The 12th Brigade advanced this morning, without opposition.
Fritz having retired some two miles further back during the night. We are billeted at Saulzoir and we expect to be held here for three or four days, in reserve.

**October 26th to 30th** We have been billeted in the village, held in reserve.
It has been very quiet for the whole five days.
The civilians have been coming back to their homes.
They have been telling us about the life they were forced to live, during the four years of the German occupation.
They were treated just like slaves.
Forced to work at bayonet point, up to their knees in water, carrying out the orders of the German officers.
Many of them have small bayonet cuts, for not working fast enough.

**October 31st** The weather is quite good considering.
At 6pm our Sergeant Major told us that Turkey have surrendered and a great cheer went up.
We are now standing to, on a minutes notice, to move up to the firing line.
Armistice was signed.

**1918 November**

**November 1st** A message came by wire at 1am that Austrian troops have surrended.
I wonder what Fritz thinks now as he is left on his own.
It has been raining heavily today.
We heard another attack start at 5am, but we have no information about it.
Orders to move up at 8am to go in support.
Moved up to support our 12th Brigade, fighting for a village named Preseau.
This village has already changed hands three times in the last forty eight hours.
We attacked at dawn in support of the 12th Brigade.
Artillery shelling was splendid, laying a continuous barrage behind the village.
It was so heavy and concentrated that the enemy had no hope of getting through it.
Fritz was caught like a rat in a trap.
We fought our way in, taking five hundred prisoners.
The barrage lifted so that we could move on.
The enemy are attempting to retire in some sort of order.
His rear-guard is providing some stiff opposition.
Orders came through that all our Divisions are to be relieved tomorrow, then go back for a rest.

**November 3rd** Held our position and were relieved by the 11th Division.
We marched back to be billeted in what is left of a small village and we had a good rest.

**November 4th** Still resting and the news came through that on the second of November, our Brigade in total captured two tanks, ten field guns, thirty one officers and six hundred and sixty other ranks, besides machine guns and trench mortar guns.

**November 5th** Standing by in reserve ready to move up to the front line to relieve.
Heard that the Austrian armistice was signed yesterday.

**November 6th** Moved up to Preseau, about ten miles, where the enemy fought such a desperate battle rear-guard action a few days ago.
We found a young French woman mutilated by the enemy.
They had cut off her right breast.
We ordered all the civilians out.
The village is now under heavy enemy artillery fire.
For some reason Fritz seems determined to hold this particular village.
Orders have come through for my leave to start early tomorrow.

**November 7th** Leave orders confirmed at 7.30am and left at 9am and marched to Athies.
Got a lift on a motor truck to Cambrai.
Entrained for Arras at 3.30pm and arrived just before midnight

**November 8th** Spent the night in Arras and entrained at 11am for Calais and set sail for Dover at 8.30am.
Reached Dover at 10.00am and London at 2.45pm.
Had a snack at a canteen and caught the 3.50pm to Birmingham, arriving at 6.35pm and eventually got home at 7.30 pm.
Went for a drink in the evening and all the talk is of our great advance.

The papers are full of reports that Marshall Ferdinand Foch has given the Germans instructions to send envoys to meet him.

**November 10th** On leave and it looks as though I shall not have to go back to France.
The Sunday papers report the Kaiser has abdicated and that the Crown Prince has given up the throne.
The Observer expects the Armistice to be signed later today.

**November 11th** Well it's all over.
The Armistice was signed in Germany at 5.00am.
Hostilities to cease at 11am.
Great rejoicing all over Birmingham – everybody has gone slightly mad with joy.

# Final Analysis

## Conclusion

At the termination of his leave Private Brooks returned to his Regiment to complete his engagement and was discharged from the Army in March 1920, having served a total of twenty years and three months with the colour and reserve.
On his return to civilian life he married Mrs Jane Rice-Jones, the widow of an ex-motorcycle despatch rider of the Royal Army Service Corps, with whom he had formed a close friendship, after the death of her husband some two years earlier.
He returned to his job as a tram driver until his health deteriorated and in 1928 was forced, much to his shame and humiliation to accept light work in the depot.
Dr. Montgomery, his medical practitioner, and the medical staff of the Birmingham General Hospital were in no doubt that the deterioration of both his stomach and lungs was a result of the after effects of wartime gassing. They fought in vain for his entitlement for a disability pension.
His health deteriorated to the extent that he was unable to work for some years and he died in poor financial circumstances, following the complete breakdown of his lungs in January 1936.

**Comments by Final Editor :**

The diary was started just before the war and ended just after the war - he did not keep any other diaries either before or after the war. In periods of crises, or rest, the dates are clumped together and during leave he made very few entries. After the war he did not discuss his wartime experiences, except the effect of the gassings.
His way of coping was to distance himself from himself by making observations and writing it down. That way he could try and forget about the war in his mind.(Catharsis) He was also a lot older than the average, with previous military experiences, which helped him to cope.
He did not try to be a Hero, but did his duty. His feeling of revenge for his friends that died kept him going, despite inadequate rest periods which actually made him more vulnerable to danger. He understood the importance of adequate trenches for protection during this particular kind of warfare.
The diary confirms that during the latter half he was quite prominent in reserve and not part of the storm troops.
His son, John Brooks, a veteran of WW2, in the Royal Air Force, wanted to publish his diaries so that his father's memory could live on, but due to lack of interested publishers, could not achieve this.
"We will remember them".

**Perspective of WW1.**

The diary reflects 3/4 of the time Private Brooks spent on his part of the front line, which consisted of one section, of a battalion, of a Division. The rest of the front line was made up by the armies of the Belgians, north west, and the French, south east, of his position. The Portuguese, the Italians and from 1917 the Americans to the south.
Towards the east of Europe were the Russians. He was however not always in the same position as he was later part of the Army corps Division and part of the reserves, which were moved around to the hot spots.
The brunt of the war took place in Europe, but the war also raged on the oceans between German U-boats and allied shipping, and in the former British Colonies, the world over.
1914 Western Front, Eastern Front, Balkan front, Turkish front, Togo-land, Cameroon, German East Africa.
1915 also included Greece, Masurian lakes, Montenegro, Suez canal.
1916 Baghdad to Basra along the Tigris river and An Nasiriya to Basra. Also the Austria-Hungarian and Italian front, Serbian-Bulgarian front, Armenian Front
1917 Romanian Front
1918 Northern Rhodesia, Portuguese East Africa, British East Africa. Palestine (Megiddo) Balkan
A large factor, not often mentioned, in the war was civilian mutinies and revolts, which took place all over Germany and the South Eastern German allied countries. i.e. political unrest.

**Casualties :**

Total casualties 37,000,000
of which 17, 000,000 deaths; 10,000,000 military; 7,000,000 civilians 20,000,000 wounded. 6,000,000 of the 10,000,000 were by Entente powers (Allied forces); 4,000,000 by Central powers.
Spanish flu caused a third of the total military deaths.
(6,000,000 went missing, presumed dead.)
UK deaths 995,939 out of 45.4 million population = 2.19% (4.38% of male population)
Germany deaths 2.050,897 out of 64.9 million population = 3.82% (7.64% of male population)

The highest mortality were amongst the :
Serbians 16.11% of total population and
Ottoman empire 13.72% of total population;
Romania 9.33% of total population.
The Global mortality : grand total were 9.722,620 military personnel 5.893,000 out of total of 954.2 million = 1.75% with 21,228,813 military wounded.

As casualties occurred amongst the most able bodied people at that time, it actually represented a ten per cent impact on the future working generation.

The figures do not add up due to differences in sources and interpretations, on how they were calculated, whether rounding up or down, but gives an approximate idea of the scale of the casualties.

It does not reflect the impact both psychological and on individual families, who had lost someone in the war, which escalated the effect of the figures tenfold.

Sources : The Viking Atlas of World War I - Anthony Livesey; and Wikipedia.

# THE END.

**References**

To confirm spelling of people and place names and locations:
Arras map 51b 1917.
The History of the First World War by David Stephenson. ISBN 0-140-26817-0
The Viking Atlas of World War One by Anthony Livesey ISBN 0-670-85372-0
Retreat and Rear-guard 1914.by Jerry Murland. ISBN 978-1-84884-391-2
Wikipedia
Google maps.

William Brooks :
Born: 16th January 1880.
Joined Royal Warwickshire Regiment: 25th November 1899
Joined war: 5th August 1914
Completed his duty: March 1920
Married Jane Rice- Jones: 12th April 1920
One son John Henry Brooks born: 30th January 1921
Died: 25th January 1936

**Movements**
**1914**
**Date Place**
Aug 5 Royal Warwickshire regiment.
Aug 8 Newport Isle of Wright.-
Aug 9 Freshwater
Aug 23 Needles Fort
Sept 1 Parkhurst
Oct 23 Le Havre
Nov 5 Armentieres
Nov 21 Between Nieppe and Ypres (7 miles from Nieppe)
Dec 13 Bailleul (La Crèche )
Dec 24 St. Yvon
Dec 29 La Crèche
Dec 30 Nieppe March to Steenwerck
**1915**
Jan 1 St Yvon (one kilometre NNE of Ploegsteert
ten miles from Nieppe)
Jan 5 La Crèche
Jan 15 Armentieres for day
Jan 20 La Crèche
Jan 22 Nieppe
Jan 24 Steenwerck hospital
Feb 1 La Crèche
Feb 6 La Crèche
Feb 22 La Crèche
Feb 23 Nieppe
Feb 27 St. Yvon
Mar 9 La Crèche
Mar 11 Nieppe
Mar 15 Armentieres
Mar 17 La Crèche
Mar 21 Wulverghem

Mar 26 La Crèche
Mar 28 Nieppe
Mar 30 Steenbecque
Apr 1 Ballyhead - Hosp  Bourlong - Rouen(Ankle sprain)
Apr 25 Ypres (Close to Wieltje)
Apr 28 Farm at Wieltje
May 8 Potiuze Château St. Julien Gas
May 14 Vlamertinghe wood
May 17 Ypres
May 22 Bourlong hospital. Gassing
May 28 Rouen
July 9 Poperinge
July 20 Houtkerque
July 22 Rail to Doullens Freschevillers 15 miles to Bertrancourt
July 25 Sucrerie near Mailly-Maillet
Aug 9 Lealvillers billet
Aug10/14 Acheux-en-amienois  park
Aug 15 Mailly-Maillet
Aug 23 Sucrerie (Near Mailly-Maillet)
Sept 10 Varennes
Sept 15 Sucrerie
Sept 23 Acheux
Sept 26 Beausart (5Km South of Doullens)
Sept 29 Marched from Beausart to Sucrerie
Oct 24 Acheux-en-amienois
Nov 21 Back from leave Mailly-Maillet
Dec 4 Forceville
Dec 14 Colincamps
Dec 22 Varennes-
Dec 30 Acheux

**1916**

Jan 1 Mailly-Maillet - firing line
Jan 10 Forceville - billets

Jan 18 Colincamps - billets
Feb 2 Colincamps
Feb 3 Montcourt for rest - 4 hours march
Mar 17 Humbercamps - firing line
Mar 20 Bienvillers - firing line
Mar 21 Monchy
Mar 17 Humbercamps
Mar 20 Bienvillers
Mar 21 Monchy
Mar 31 Humbercamps 3 miles behind
Apr 7 Bienvillers
Apr 24 Monchy
May 1 St Amand 10 miles to Halloy
May 3 Marched to Neuvillette via Doullens
May 5 Marched to Agenville 20Km
May 20 (12 Km) to Gapennes
June 4 (22 Km) Fienvillers
June 5 Fienvillers to Warnimont wood
June 11 Bertrancourt
June 13 Mailly-Maillet
June 18 Auchonvillers

**Somme**

July 1 Beaumont Hamel
July 8 Wood off Mailly-Maillet Forceville Rd.
July 19 Camp off Bertrancourt – Acheux Rd.
July 20 March to Beauval
July 22 March to Candas
July 23 Entrained to Poperinge (Ypres)
July 27 Rations from La Brique
Aug 3 Vlamertinghe billets
Aug 11 Boesinghe firing line
Aug 13/14 Trois Tours firing line
Aug 15 Château Brielen

Aug 21 Poperinge Hill 60 firing line
Aug 31 Marched 13 Km to Vlamertinghe-Oudenaarde Rd
Sept 4 Near Poperinge on Proven Rd
Sept 17 Marched to Proven entrained via Calais, Boulogne to Amiens Marched 13 Km to Colsy
Sept 18 Marched 13 Km to Corbie
Sept 25 Marched to Mericourt
Sept 30 Marched to Daours
Oct 7 Marched to Meaulte
Oct 8 Mansel camp near Mametz
Oct 9 Two days travel to firing line near. La Transloy and Les Boeufs
Oct 12 Battle Transloy ridge - Bapaume
Oct 13 Guillemont
Oct 17 Bernafay wood
Oct 23 Battle Ancre Heights-Moved to east of Les Boeufs
Oct 24 Trones wood
Oct 25 Rest camp near Mametz
Oct 27 Entrained for Corbie to rest
Oct 30 Entrained for Airnes - marched 20 Km to Huppy
Nov 1 Billets at Huppy
Nov 18 On Leave one month-Le Havre
Dec 23 Back from leave
Dec 27 Sallisel
Dec 30 Five miles by lorry to Bray for billets

**1917**

(Training at Bray until Jan 14)
Jan 16 Camp near Suzanne? - lorry to Bouchavesnes
Jan 24 Marched 18 Km
Jan 25 Marched back 10 Km to Suzanne (hutted camp) rest
Feb 2 Reserve trenches
Feb 10 Bouchavesnes firing line
Feb 17 Reserve trenches

Feb 27 General reserve marched to Chipilly-Triplane
Mar 4 (4 day march) 10 Km to Corbie
Mar 5 (21 Km) to Villers-Bocage
Mar 6 (12 Km) to Beauval
Mar 7 (14 Km) to Mezerolles
Mar 12 Move to Arras area
Mar 13 Marched 19 Km to Rebreuve
Mar 14 Marched 20 Km to Savy (2Km from Aubigny)
Mar 18 Special training
Mar 21 (20 Km) to Camblain Châtelaine
Mar 24 Marles to visit friend
Apr 2 ? Vimy ridge
Apr 5/6 (16 Km). to Bethouart
Apr 8 Marched to X-camp south of Ecoivres near Arras
Apr 9 Battle of Arras (At St Nicholas near Arras) 4 mile advance to Fampoux
Apr 13 Reserve trenches
Apr 16 Firing line just left of Fampoux
Apr 21 Rest St Nicholas Lorry to Beaufort
Apr 23 St Ambrines
Apr 28 Y camp near Arras
Apr 30 Trenches just left of Fampoux
May 3 Battle of the Scarpe
May 6 Railway embankment
May 11/12 Arras final stages. 7am took Roux Cemetery & Chemical works
May 13 Blue line rest Motor transport to Houvin Houvigneul For Battle training
June 11 Move by lorry to Arras in reserve
June 19 Firing line
June 23 Relieved to Stirling camp
July 1 Firing line
July 5 Relieved Dingwall camp

July 7 Laurent Blangy
July 13 To Arras
July 16 Support in firing line
July 21 Leave break to St Valery
Aug 5 Near Blangy
Aug 8 Firing line Left of Monchy
Aug 15 To right of Loos
Aug 19 Relieved into reserve, meeting Percy at Arras station.
Aug 24 Digging party Blangy
Aug 25 Bath at Candle factory St. Nicholas
Aug 26 Firing line 2 hour march.
Sept 3 Relieved
Sept 4 Went visiting to Arras
Sept 6 Moved off 2nd stop at Achicourt to Bailleval.
Sept 7 Battle training
Sept 19 Railhead 1h 45m march - Entrain in trucks to Proven.
Sept 27 Entrain at Elverdinge near Ypres -March to camp at Breary (?Brielen) in reserve
Oct 4 Broodseinde Second wave between 29 Div and 11th Brigade
Oct 7 Rest
Oct 9-13 Firing line- Line of shell holes Passchendale
Oct 14 Rest Jolly farm air bombing
Oct 15 K-camp Poperinge
Oct 17 To Poperinge Entrain for Aubigny Marched to Y-camp at Etrun 8 Km from Arras (Hazebrouck on the way)
Oct 23 Achicourt near Arras
Oct 24 Trenches on reserve
Nov 1 (2nd) line
Nov 5 Firing line
Nov 9 Relieved to Arras on Cambrai Rd
Nov 15 On special leave train from Arras
Nov 16 Boulogne to London

Nov 30 Back from leave Boulogne St Martins camp
Dec 1 To Arras on reserve
Dec 10 Wilderness on Arras - Cambrai Rd.Assembly trenches
Dec 13 Chalk pits Feuchy - Chapel crossroads
Dec 14 Trenches near Monchy
Dec 26 Support line
Dec 29 Four day rest Camp near Arras

**1918**

Jan 3 Close support Foss farm
Jan 7 Firing line Trenches collapsing
Jan 15 To firing line
Jan 16 Trenches unserviceable
Jan 18 On top due to mud (both sides)
Jan 19 To 2nd line
Jan 21 Tilloy
Jan 22 To Arras for 4 day rest training
Jan 27 2nd line just north of Arras Cambrai Rd.
Feb 4 Relieved to Arras - Rest training
Mar 5 In reserve
Mar 19 Reserve trenches Ludendorff's offensive
Mar 22 Fighting -Monchy lost
Mar 31 To attack
Apr 2 Relieved to 600yards back in reserve trench.
Apr 5 2nd reserve line
Apr 8 Relieved - to Blangy locks 5 miles on St Pol Rd, other side of Arras.
Apr 9 One mile away near to Agnes Duisans
Apr 11 Just outside Agnes Duisans
Apr 12 Lillers near La Bassee
Apr 15 To attack. Pontoon bridge Picault wood
Apr 18 Relieved to reserve - old château

Apr 20 Standing by in reserve Gonnehem close to front line (milk cow)
Apr 23 Moved up in support old barn
Apr 25 Trench digging - horses killed
Apr 29 Cellar
May 1 Kind of fever
May 2 Reserve Busnettes
May 3 Villa
May 6 To move up to firing line shell holes
May 15 Relieved to Busnettes
May 19 Firing line dugout digging
May 27 Relieved - to Busnettes
June 2 Firing line Trenches between Gonnehem and Robecq short of Hinges, just north of Bethune.
June 15 Back in reserve
June 16 Working party
June 19 Firing line - more fever cases, capture prisoners with iron cross
July 1 Relieved - Busnettes
July 7 Firing line - horse flies and mosquitoes
July 12 Digging party at trench
July 21 Relieved - Busnettes
July 26 Firing line
July 28 Scouting Robecq
Aug 2 Dugout digging for winter
Aug 7 Enemy retreating Acher wood - good advance
Aug 24 Relieved - Perns St Eloie – French wine
Aug 28 Firing line - (= advancing on Hindenburg line)
Sept 3 Reserve to captured enemy trench Arras Cambrai Rd.
Sept 4 To Bailleul-aux-Cornailles (8 Km from St. Pol) for rest
Sept 6 Escort of prisoner from Coyecques 30 miles off via Aire (Cathedral)

Sept 18 Trenches Tinges - Monchy 5 miles from Arras Right of Eglaine front of Dury village Dam of River Scarpe. 25 mile advance on 40 mile front

Sept 25 Moved into reserve

Sept 27 Reserve trench standing by

Oct 4 In reserve

Oct 6 Relieved (Arras in museum)

Oct 7 Marched 11 Km to Simecourt for rest

Oct 11 To Move marched 2 miles Buses to Rollancourt from where they marched to one mile this side of Cambrai

Oct 12 Marched N-E from there

Oct 13 In pursuit of enemy Naves for rest

Oct 18 Relieving Dukes at Villers-De-Couche

Oct 21 Saulzoir

Oct 25 Billeted at Saulzoir

Oct 31 Standing to

Nov 1 Preseau

Nov 3 Relieved

Nov 5 Standing by in reserve

Nov 6 Moved up to Preseau

Nov 7 Leave order Marched to Athies Lift to Cambrai Entrain for Arras

Nov 8 Calais Dover London Birmingham

Nov 11 Armistice.

# People Names:

"Spud" Pte. ..........................................1916 Jan Mar,
Streeton Lieut. (Killed in action)................... 1918.May11
Summers, "Tich" Pte. (wounded)................. 1915Mar25,
"Threshy" Pte. ........................................... 1915 Dec.
Toby Pte. ............................................ 1914 Nov Dec.
Tynsdale, Cpl. ......... 1915 Dec (Shell shocked 1916Mar3)
Walters R.R. Lieut. ..................................... .1916 Jul.
Warren D.A. Capt. ..................................... 1917 May.
Watkins "Daddy" Pte.(Killed in Action) .1916 Feb 1917 Oct.3
Watson "Tiddly" Pte. .................................. 1917 Sep.
Whitehouse Cpl. ....................................... 1915 Dec.
Williams Sgt.(Killed in action) .................... 1917Jun21.
Willis D.H. Lieut. ........................................ 1916 Mar.
Wilson "Tug" Pte. ...................................... 1918 Jul.

## Place names

| Place | Date(s) mentioned in Diary |
|---|---|
| Acheux-en-amienois | 1915 Aug, Sept, Oct, Nov, Dec, 1916 Jul. |
| Achicourt | 1917 Sept, Oct. |
| Agenville | 1916 May. |
| Aire | 1818 Sept. |
| Airaines | 1916 Oct. |
| Agnez-les-Duisans | 1918 Apr. |
| Ambrines | 1917 Apr. |
| Amiens | 1916 Sep. |
| Ancre | 1916 Oct. |
| Arleux | 1917 Apr. |
| Armentieres | 1914 Nov. 1915 Jan Mar. |
| Arras | 1917 Apr, May, June, July, Oct, Dec, 1918 Jan, Feb, Oct, Nov. |
| Artois | 1915 Mar, 1917 Apr. |
| Athies | 1918 Nov. |
| Aubigny En Artois | 1917 Mar, Oct. |
| Auchonvillers | 1916 June. |
| Authie | 1916 June |
| Bailleul | 1918 Sept. |
| Bailleval | 1917 Mar, Sept. |
| Ballyhead | 1915 Mar. |
| Bapaume | 1916 Oct. |
| La Bassee | 1915 Oct. |
| Beaufort | 1917 Apr. |
| Beaumont Hamel | 1916 July, Oct. |
| Beausart | 1915 Sept. |
| Beauval | 1916 July. 1917 Mar. |
| Bernafay wood | 1916 Oct. |
| Les Beoufs | 1916 Oct. |
| Bertrancourt | 1915 July 1916 June, July. |

Sailly-Sallisel.....................1916 Dec.
Saulzoir............................1918 Oct.
Savy (near Albigny)...........1917 Mar.
Scarpe............................. 1917 May, Sept. 1918 Mar.
Simecourt village............... 1918 Oct.
Steenbecque..................... 1915 Mar.
Steenwerck.......................1914 Dec 1915 Jan.
Stirling camp ....................1917 June.
Suzanne............................1917 Jan.
Tilloy................................1918 Jan.
Tincques...........................1918 June, Sept.
Le Transloy........................1916 Oct.
Trois Tours........................1916 Aug, Nov.
Trones wood......................1916 Oct.
Varennes...........................1915 Sept, Dec.
Verdun..............................1914 Nov. 1916 July.
Villers-Bocage....................1917 Mar.
Villers-De-Couche (Coucy-La-Ville)..1918 Oct.
Vimy ridge near Arras..........1917 Apr.
Vlamertinghe......................1915 May. 1916 Aug 1917 Sept.
Wieltje..............................1915 Mar.
Watao Rd...........................1916 July.
Wilderness camp ................1917 Dec.
Wulverghem.......................1915 Mar.
Ypres...................1914 Nov. 1915 Mar, May. 1916 Jul.
1917 Sep.

## Abbreviations used in this book :

ANZAC...........Australian and New Zealand Army Corps
A.S.C.............Army Service Corps
A.W.O.L.........Absent with-out Leave
B.E.F..............British Expeditionary Force
Btn................Battalion
Brig...............Brigadier
Capt..............Captain
Col................Colonel
Cmdr..............Commander
Coy................Company
Cpl................Corporal
DCM .............Distinguished Conduct Medal.
Div................Division
D.S.O............ Distinguished Service Order (medal)
Gen...............General
H.Q...............Headquarters
ISBN..............International Standard Book Number
L/Cpl.............Lance Corporal
Lancs............Lancaster Regiment
Lincolns.........Lincolnshire Regiment
Lt/Lieut..........Lieutenant
Maj...............Major
Minnies..........minenwerfers (Mortar)
NCO...............Non Commissioned Officer.
OBE...............Order of the British Empire award.
Pte................Private
R.A.M.C..........Royal Army Medical Corps.
Regt..............Regiment
R.I.F..............Royal Irish Fusiliers
R.I.R..............Royal Irish Rifle Brigade
RMS...............Royal Merchant Ship

RSM...............Regimental Sergeant Major
RWR..............Royal Warwickshire Regiment.
sap...............Covered Trench.
Sgt...............Sergeant
St. ...............Saint
T.A. .............Territorial Army.

estaminet......Wine shop.

www.ingramcontent.com/pod-product-compliance
Lightning Source LLC
Chambersburg PA
CBHW051814090426
42736CB00011B/1480
*9780957648906*